Praise for The Social Media Job Search Workbook

"Joshua makes social media accessible. He explains not only what but how and why. This guidebook will help you understand the dynamics of how to use social media for career management."

— Martin Yate CPC,
NY Times bestseller Knock 'em Dead

"Joshua expertly demonstrates how anyone can tame the wild west of social media to land that next job through mindful planning and deliberate action."

— Michael "Dr. Woody" Woodward, PhD
Organizational psychologist and author of the Amazon top-selling job-hunting book The YOU Plan

"Joshua has done it again! He's created the perfect companion to Job Search with Social Media for Dummies in this workbook. It's a focused, actionable and results-oriented tool for using social media to find work—fast!"

— Kevin Kermes,
founder and editor of Career Attraction

"Joshua's workbook fills a huge gap in how we understand and utilize social media. Not only is this an excellent resource for active job seekers, but also for those who want to build their personal brands throughout their careers. Anyone serious about their career should get this book."

— Pete Leibman,
Author of I Got My Dream Job and So Can You

THE
SOCIAL MEDIA
JOB SEARCH
WORKBOOK

By Joshua Waldman

With Dr. Sean Harry

For permission requests, write to the publisher, addressed "Attention: Permissions Coordinator," at the address below. Career Enlightenment LLC13500 SW Pacific Hwy Ste 101Tigard, OR 97223Or send an email through: www.careerenlighten-ment.com

Photo Credits: All photos are under a creative commons attribution license thanks to Flickr.com. Oprah Winfrey photo by Alan LightHoward Stern photo by B. NortonSteve Jobs photo by Segagman

Book design: Otto Dimitrijevics

Cover design: Kris Taft Miller of KT Design, LLC

This Book Belongs to

 _____

My First Tweet (140 Characters)

_____

_____

_____

Foreword to the 2015 Edition

In a year, there's been plenty of user interface changes with our favorite three social media tools, LinkedIn, Facebook and Twitter.

For instance, LinkedIn has implemented in-line editing, better news delivery and cover images for premium profiles. Facebook has revamped their search results pages making it easier to find past posts. Twitter's interface continues to improve in small ways making it more pleasing to navigate and manage the flow of information.

Yet despite these apparent updates, fundamental principles still apply. The frameworks contained in this book were only affected in so far as needing updated screenshots. You'll still use the same, tried-and-true strategies for informational interviewing and crafting your message.

So what's new in this edition, besides new screenshots?

- Expanded discussion questions for the second two parts of the book. I felt that the exercises in the back of the book lacked the same level of interactivity as the Personal Branding chapters. You'll find the flow for the Polishing and Publishing sections more engaging.

- The introduction of my LinkedIn profile grading tool:http://profilegrade.com. This online tool will tell you exactly what's wrong with your profile and provide suggestions for improvement.

- I've redesigned the inside of the book to make it easier to navigate. Bolder chapter headings, easier to fill out exercises, and clearer graphics should make running through this program more fun.

Since last year, Career Enlightenment, my company and the imprint for this book, has enjoyed remarkable success. I am ever grateful to be able to do what I love and also pay my bills!

- We've expanded our LinkedIn profile writing services, added new people to the team and doubled our sales: http://liprofile.com

- I've launched a profile writing certification program for resume writers to improve the overall quality of profiles written by resume writers: http://careerenlightenment.com/lipw

- The DoL funded employment office in Portland released a very compelling white paper about the social media job search course I designed and currently teach: http://careerenlightenment.com/whitepaper

- We completely redesigned our webpage so that it's easier to read across all devices, desktop and mobile: http://careerenlightenment.com

- This very workbook has been adopted across the country at various schools as part of their training curriculum for students about to enter the workforce.

Of course, I'm excited to see what this year brings. One of the best parts of doing what I do is that nothing stays the same, it's always changing, forcing me to stay on my toes and adapt.

I hope this year's workbook will serve you well and help you find that job you've always wanted.

—Joshua Waldman

Portland, Oregon, January 2015

Foreword to the 2014 Edition

In just one year, since the publication of this book's first edition, the landscape of social media has changed.

- All three of the major social networks have gone public. Twitter (TWTR) joined Facebook (FB) and LinkedIn (LNKD) in the public markets. All three stocks have outperformed trader expectations.

- New strategic directions with LinkedIn have improved their user interface while stripping features from free and low-tier paid users. LinkedIn's Thought Leader applications and newsfeed improvements have turned the platform into a place that many more people now turn to for daily news and advice.

- Facebook has reduced the reach that a brand's Page has on individual feeds, slashing traffic and angering Internet marketers worldwide. Facebook's message, "You've gotta pay to play," all in the name of improving the user experience, continues to drive major changes to the platform. Meanwhile, Facebook's Graph Search has changed the game for recruiters, who can now tap into almost 1 billion user profiles for sourcing with third-party applications built just for them.

This year, in front of over 50 college academic advisors at the University of Illinois, I demonstrated how to research Skills on LinkedIn. And I learned yet again how often these features change. The page on LinkedIn I wanted to demonstrate, the page I had double-checked the day before this presentation, had been taken down. "Well, ladies and gentlemen," I said, "we won't be researching Skills anymore."

Despite inevitable changes like this, the basic principles in this book remain the same. In fact, these changes underline the importance of focusing not on features but on frameworks.

All that you will learn here—the Three P's, the FIRE Method, the 20-Minute Ritual and so forth, were designed to weather the tempest of social media's adolescence. Yes, I've improved this 2014 edition. I've expanded some areas that needed it and even had to respond to the technology changes in the explanations of certain steps. But in their essence these principles are no different now from when I first developed them, and they will continue to serve you in your career success for years to come.

One major improvement from the 2013 edition of this workbook is the new use of online video to augment certain instructions.

 You'll find this symbol throughout the text. Follow it to get step-by-step video instructions for the activity I'm describing.

As many of my readers also work with career coaches or LinkedIn profile writers as they read this, I've indicated certain areas worth sharing with your career guide with this symbol:

Finally, you'll find a much expanded personal branding section with even more insight-building activities.

Today's job seekers cannot avoid the implications of social media on their career's success or failure. There will be those who will choose to ignore it and wonder why they aren't making much progress. Then there are you, who've chosen to do something different than the generations before you. You've chosen to respond to these societal changes. I hope the principles in this book continue to serve you and make you successful.

— Joshua Waldman

Portland, Oregon, January 2014

Foreword to 2013 Edition

It's March 2009. I'm sitting in a small conference room in an office complex in Lake Oswego, Oregon, also known as Silicon Forest, Oregon's version of Silicon Valley. My manager had called me into a meeting to "review my quarter." But the quarter wasn't finished and there was something in his voice.

I found him sitting in the room with our operations manager, who was never involved in sales meetings. That's when I knew. But it still stung. The papers on the desk facing me were my severance terms, not my quarterly report. I remember the apology in his voice when he confessed, "You've probably guessed that this isn't a meeting to review your sales. I'm sorry." Somehow everything in the room got much sharper. The smell of recycled air, the muffled murmurings of phone calls down the hallway, all became sharp, distinct, and painful.

This day in March marked the beginning of a very dark period for me, indeed for the whole country. Six months earlier, Cisco had laid me off with thousands of others in what we now call the "economic downturn of 2008." With a Master's degree and years of experience, I couldn't reconcile the belief I had held since I was a freshman at Brown University— that a good education would provide me all of the opportunities I would ever need in life—with the poverty of my present situation.

I was defeated. I gave the companies I worked for all control over my financial and emotional life, and in return, they turned me out. Although I didn't know it at the time, this series of layoffs turned out to be the best thing that ever happened to me.

The period of unemployment after Lake Oswego forced me to evaluate my career and my life. Almost all of my professional opportunities had come from someone I knew. I either networked my way into jobs or was referred into them. Another interesting theme was my involvement with newer technologies, from distributing solar panels in Nepal to selling digital academic journals in Boston. So with a new self-awareness, I resolved to use social networking to figure out how to get my next job. Great thing was, it worked. I networked online like crazy, spending hours a day perfecting my profiles, researching companies, and reaching out to professionals in jobs I admired. They met with me, guided me, and referred me. Soon, I discovered I could get job interviews just by using the strategies I discovered.

I began to blog about what I learned, writing almost daily, and my following grew. This opened up opportunities with Wiley, who published my first book, Job Searching with Social Media For Dummies, one of the top-selling titles in that series. I've traveled the world, training professionals on career advancement strategies. I've helped hundreds of career advisors overcome their confusion about social media so they can better serve their clients and students.

In the moment, sometimes life can feel pretty hopeless, without choices. But when I look back at 2008 and 2009, I did have choices. And from those choices I learned the joy of public speaking, enthusiasm for writing, and resourcefulness at researching better uses of new technology. Thank you, corporate America, for showing me who I really am.

I believe it's time for people to stop giving away all of their personal power to corporations. I believe it's time for you to own your body of work, to own your brand, to own the responsibility for where you are working and will work and how you will work. This workbook is dedicated to you and your path to regain control over your career. Because you shouldn't have to get laid off to learn this lesson.

—Joshua Waldman

Portland, Oregon, January 2013

How to Use This Book

This book offers you a plan. Designed to interact with you, it can be used to record your thoughts and guide your online activities one step at a time. So please follow the order of activities this book presents, even if you think a step is not important. Believe me, it is.

I wrote this workbook to give job seekers like you a hands-on complement to the reference books on the market (like the one I wrote, Job Searching with Social Media For Dummies). Reference books are the place to look for full descriptions of each type of social media, definitions, etc. This workbook picks up where those books leave off in its linearity. Use this workbook when you're ready to move from understanding to action!

> ❝This workbook picks up where those books leave off. Use this workbook when you're ready to move from understanding to action!❞

This workbook picks up where those books leave off. Use this workbook when you're ready to move from understanding to action!

I intentionally refrain from asking you to "go online and do this and that." I ask you, for example, to write down your first tweet on paper. I then ask you to write down your LinkedIn headline and summary, again, on paper. This is by design.

Don't Touch That Computer…Yet

In training these topics over the years, I've found that writing things down on paper first can produce better results then immediately posting them online particularly when you are new to these tools. I highly advise you to wait until you're done with the activities in the workbook before you transfer your writings to the appropriate online channel. Jot down your answers in the spaces provided here, not online…not yet.

(Besides, new research shows that writing things down actually helps you learn better than typing!)

Don't Spend Too Much Time Here

How quickly and intensely you go through this workbook is up to you. However, I find that spending more than an hour a day will cause you to feel overwhelmed. Just like learning a language, it's often better to spend a little bit of time every day than to put in a lot of time every once in a while. If you want to get hired fast, then resolve to work through this workbook 30 to 60 minutes a day, which should take you about a week to go through all the reading and activities here.

What If I Get Stuck

 In this workbook, you will find this symbol throughout the text. Follow that link provided to watch a free instructional video showing you exactly how to perform that task. If you get stuck, this is the place to go for help. If you want to share the video with a friend (or client), you are welcome to do so as well.

If there are areas where you are getting stuck and you would like me to produce a video instruction for you, please let me know by contacting me here: *http://careerenlightenment.com.* I will read your email and will put your request in my queue. I promise, I read every email.

Use This Book to Support Your Work with Your Career Professional

If you choose to work with a career coach, LinkedIn writer or resume writer, consider sharing your answers from this book's exercises with your career professional to help them understand you better. In fact, I ask my own clients, who hire me to write their LinkedIn profiles, to share elements from these exercises so my writers better understand them and write in their voice.

To learn more about my LinkedIn profile writing services and receive a special offer as a workbook reader, visit *http://liprofile.com*

 I will indicate which parts of this workbook are worth sharing with your coach or writer using this symbol.

A Note to Instructors

If you train job seekers at any level—college, unemployed, military re-entry, etc.—you may benefit from reading the companion Instructor's Manual to this workbook, which includes syllabus, handouts, and companion slides for the classroom.

To learn how to get a copy of the Instructor's Manual, visit *http://careerenlightenment.com/facilitators*.

To download a free copy of the syllabus that I have developed to go with this workbook in my own four-hour training sessions, visit *http://careerenlightenment.com/syllabus*.

Contents

List of Excercises

Introduction

Many classes that promise to teach LinkedIn skills for job seekers fail to address the most important issue: what you actually say online. Yes, it may feel helpful to sit in a classroom and learn where to click. But if what you are posting about yourself is not supported by some strategy, your profiles—although 100% complete—will appear inconsistent and not compelling to business decision-makers. Learning where to click in LinkedIn is useless if you haven't put serious thought into what you will actually say.

What's more, many career professionals have pulled together their information from free online sources, such as YouTube, free webinars, or blog posts, and some of these sources offer dubious advice or outdated technical information.

> **Today, simply having a profile isn't good enough. Your profile has to be amazing.**

This workbook isn't about your technical education. It's about fitting the pieces together so that you have clear steps to finding a job. If you are looking for technical information about each of these social media tools, check out *http://grovo.com* for professionally produced 60-second instructional videos. Most of Grovo's videos are free and get updated regularly. I've listed many other technical resources at the back of this workbook as well.

In short, what you will do in this workbook cannot be found for free online somewhere else.

Today, simply having a profile isn't enough. Your profile has to be amazing. Recruiters spend on average eight seconds looking at one profile. Eight seconds! Your message needs to grab their attention immediately.

How? By following three Ps:

1) **Positioning:** discovering what makes you unique and relevant in the marketplace to position yourself as unique and valuable

2) **Polishing:** communicating your personal value on all the right channels for a polished online reputation

3) **Publishing:** requesting engagement opportunities with people of influence by posting your brand message

This workbook is based on this three P's model and will serve as your overarching social media job search framework in the pages ahead. Despite an ever-changing technology landscape, this framework can be used as your navigational sextant. And if used as instructed, it will prevent you from ever feeling overwhelmed or confused by new technology again.

Technology Will Not Save Our World

Most Americans are familiar with social media. Facebook has become the modern-day smoke break. And Twitter gets referenced in popular news media every day. President Obama presented his fall 2011 town hall meeting from LinkedIn's campuses in Mountain View, CA. Even the Pope (or someone from his office) tweets from the Vatican!

The challenges many people have with using social media to accomplish a specific goal (get a job, recruit a candidate, market a product) isn't a lack of familiarity with the individual technologies. Rather, most people struggle bringing them all together into a single, comprehensive strategy with clear goals and steps. It's not about the tool; it's how you use it. As one workshop attendee told me, "I'm not new to social media. I've been using it for years. But today, you are really putting all the pieces together for me. The tools finally all fit together."

The belief that technology can solve our problems can be traced back to the Renaissance. But as the 20th-century economist E. F. Schumacher put it, modern instantaneous communications can also destroy our personal freedoms "by making everything extremely vulnerable and extremely insecure, unless – please note – unless…conscious action is taken to mitigate the destructive effects of these technological developments."

In today's post-modern society, people somehow feel that the technologies available to them are not just a panacea for their boredom but also their inevitable right to possess and use. Just look at the number of poor LinkedIn profiles ("Oh, I'll just set up a profile quickly and wait for the jobs to roll in") or the volume of inappropriate Facebook posts with unintended consequences ("I have a right to be myself on Facebook, don't I?"). Facebook firings mount as indignant workers cry foul. Victims in these cases mistakenly blame their snoopy bosses rather than concede that their own use of technology was the real villain.

I implore you—yes, strong words—to face the fact that how you use technology matters more than the technology itself. As Schumacher put it so concisely back in the 1970s, take "conscious action" with regards to technology, and your opportunities in life can grow. Use the technologies with no plan or purpose at your own peril. I've seen too many people throw their hands up in the air in frustration at how LinkedIn "doesn't work." To their delight, often all they need are small changes to their strategy, and they get hired.

So, Why Social Media for Job Search?

Because most jobs are unlisted, networking online has become more important than ever. Tens of millions of Americans say their jobs came from social networks. Meanwhile, job boards like Monster continue to lose market share. Anyone who has been out of the job search for the last year or two will feel considerable culture shock when starting a search today.

If you are interested, see my collection of infographics on how today's companies are hiring and how people are finding work. The data may shock you: *http://careerenlightenment.com/job-search-infographics*

For instance:

92% of companies say they use LinkedIn, Facebook, and/or Twitter to hire. [Jobvite, "State of Recruiting", 2012]

- Of those, 89% use LinkedIn and 26% use Facebook. [ibid]

- 1 in six Americans say that social media helped them find work; that's tens of millions of jobs. [ibid]

- Of those jobs, 78% came from Facebook. [ibid]

- The number of recruiters successfully using social media to hire increased by 15% over the last three years, from 58% to 73%. [Jobvite, "State of Recruiting", 2013]

Despite these facts, many job seekers still fixate on job boards and resumes as their primary tools. For them, social media "doesn't work" because they've put only a fraction of their attention on using it. While they wait for the magic results to happen (they are using technology after all!), they get frustrated. Those who show a willingness to use social networking seriously and as the main control room for their career get results fast, as you are about to find out.

Remember that social media is a publishing medium. When you use it, you are a publisher. You must think about the image you are portraying and how it will impact your life. It would be a mistake to start using social networking technologies without first considering your personal brand. And so that's what you are going to learn first.

Why Start with Personal Branding?

I taught my first LinkedIn class in 2006, the year I graduated with an MBA from Boston University. At that point, LinkedIn wasn't well studied or even widely adopted. Mostly, people considered it, at best, an optional tool for storing their resume online and, at worst, an annoying invitation emailed by a co-workers who should be doing their job.

Back then, our focus was on the features of the tool. "Look, you can have a professional summary, oh wow!" Or "Look how easy it is to send an email to a fellow alum."

> 66 **The only way to accomplish the kind of clear, powerful, job-attracting message that will separate you from all the other candidates is to develop a compelling, thoughtful, intentional personal brand.** 99

Nowadays, such a feature-based orientation is less than helpful. First, anyone can learn these features from YouTube or Grovo.com. Second, telling someone "Look, here is where you put your professional headline" is useless if that person doesn't know what he or she should say.

In other words, message first, medium second.

If you've felt overwhelmed when it comes to how you show up online, then chances are you've had the wrong focus—a focus on the features of the tool.

I start you off here by shifting that focus back to you, your message, your goals, your plan. To put it simply, I help you with what to put in those blank spaces. Because the only way to accomplish the kind of clear, powerful, job-attracting message that will separate you from all the other candidates is to develop a compelling, thoughtful, intentional personal brand.

Limitations of This Book

LinkedIn, Facebook, and Twitter dominate the social media world here in the United States. Their prevalence in the world of job search makes them essential for study. However, in other countries, in certain niche markets other social networks can be very useful.

This book will only focus on these three networks. However, the strategies and principles here can apply to any social network. Courses dealing with other social networks can still use these frameworks and strategies, although some technical details will, of course, be different.

Part 1

Position Yourself

What Is Personal Positioning?

You've probably heard of personal branding. There are two main problems with this term. First, it's overused, to the point where it has lost its original meaning. Many people see personal branding as "image," which is only a small part of it. Second, the term branding has so many definitions as to make it almost meaningless.

Branding expert and author Barbara Findlay Schenck told me in 2012, "Your brand is whatever mental image those in your target audience automatically unlock when they encounter your name or logo. Your brand is what they believe about you based on everything they've ever seen or heard—whether good or bad, true or untrue."

Brand yourself or be branded.

Traditional brands we are familiar with come from huge corporations with hefty advertising and marketing budgets. But brands apply to individuals, too.

In 1997, Tom Peters wrote an article called "The Brand Called You" for Fast Company, where he said, "You don't belong to any company for life, and your chief affiliation isn't to any particular function. You're not defined by your job title, and you're not confined by your job description." With the average time in a company now about two years, and with the freely available tools of the Internet, personal branding these days is a given.

> "Personal branding" was first coined by Tom Peters in 1997 in an article for Fast Company called "The Brand Called You." His main point was to empower mid-level executives to run their careers like a business, i.e., to be the CEO of their own Me, Inc.

Brand yourself or be branded.

Over the last 10+ years, many personal branding models have emerged. Many of them do a great job helping job seekers understand their drives, their unique abilities, and so forth. However, few address the real power of a brand: how it is perceived by the target audience.

Your brand is the promise you make to possible employers about the value you can bring to them or their organization. Often, the part of a brand that's about them—the most important part—is missing.

You're not defined by your job title, and you're not confined by your job description.

— Tom Peters

Here you will learn the You|Them model of personal branding. You will go through a series of introspective exercises to elicit your values, passions, and drives. Then you will research or brainstorm the needs of your target organizations.

When you finally craft your positioning messages, you will know how to make them 1) congruent with who you are and 2) relevant to your target organization.

 To learn more about personal branding, watch:
http://careerenlightenment.com/personal-branding-lecture

Building Brand YOU

Of course, you don't create a personal brand from scratch. You already have one.

Don't believe it? Google your name followed by your hometown. If you have a Facebook page or LinkedIn profile, your name probably comes up on the first results page. Perhaps you are listed in a phone book. Maybe you have recently been mentioned in a local news article. If I were to ask your friends what word they would describe you with, that's your brand, too.

What you can do is manage your personal brand so that what people see about you is what you want them to see.

Even without a hefty marketing budget, there's plenty you can do to build a brand. Imagine glancing at the face of someone you admire. Notice your response. Now imagine invoking a similar response when a hiring manager sees your picture.

Exercise 1: Can You Identify These Personal Brands?

Fill in the blanks for each celebrity photo below. Doing so will help you understand the split second it takes for someone to react to your brand. You can't help your response, but the celebrity can control his or her brand. This happens when people see you too!

What comes to mind when you see this person?

ex. Rags to riches

_____

_____

_____

What comes to mind when you see this person?

Ex. Controversial

_____

_____

_____

What comes to mind when you see this person?

Ex. innovative but kind of a jerk too

_____

_____

_____

Exercise 2: Take These Online Assessments

Below is a list of online assessments. These tests can be fun to take and often reveal interesting things about yourself and the choices you make in life. Although you don't have to take these, the more of them you do, the deeper insight you will have about who you are and what makes you happy. Try a few, and record your results here.

Completing this exercise thoughtfully will help you build a personal brand that gets you where you want to go.

Consider sharing this exercise with your career coach, resume writer or professional LinkedIn profile writer. To learn about my LinkedIn profile writing services, visit *http://liprofile.com*

Assessment	URL	Your Results
The Via Survey	http://www.viame.org	
The Holland Assessment	http://bit.ly/ZcZVLr	
The MAPP Assessment	http://bit.ly/MAPP-test	
5 Min DISC Test	http://bit.ly/WKXgpQ	
My Plan Career Values	http://bit.ly/VilWoJ	
Standout	http://bit.ly/VU4QQs	
Core Values Index	http://bit.ly/corevaluesindex	
Kiersey	http://www.keirsey.com	
Trait Marker	http://traitmarker.com/	
Birkman	http://www.birkman.com/	
Strength Finder	http://careerenlightenment. com/upenn-assessments	

YOU: Discovering Your Value

Once, I was asked by a blog reader, "Should I put 'I'm looking for work' in my LinkedIn headline?" It's a common question actually. You'd be surprised how many people ask it of career professionals.

The inherent problem with this approach is that it's "me" focused. If a company wants to hire you, it's because of what they want. So lead with the value you can bring to other people.

How can you discover exactly what that value is? The following exercises challenge you to develop your "what can I do for you" mentality.

> **If a company wants to hire you, it's because of what they want.**

When you look for a job, often you must confront your deepest demons. For example, if you don't believe you have anything of value to offer, no one else will. Will you take the challenge and confront that limiting belief?

I did just that during my second layoff. And as much as the job search was practical, it was also deeply spiritual. What is my worth? Am I worthy? Do I matter? Who am I really?

These next exercises are very practical for helping you get hired. Please also take them seriously for they will help guide your introspection and personal growth as well.

Your Personality Traits

If you were a senior software engineer in Silicon Valley, where there are thousands of others with those same skills, why would a company hire you over someone else?

The answer is the same for why anyone does anything: for emotional reasons. Said simply, they'll hire you because they like you. That's it.

> **Your personality needs to shine through, particularly when you're online.**

Job seekers often make the mistake of tucking their personality away when engaging with potential employers. Their answers are formal, their written language is professional (dull), and they don't say anything that could be offensive.

The problem is that by being "professional" and not showing your personality, you become a commodity. There are others more experienced, more skilled, or more educated than you going for the same jobs you want. And if these were the only factors, you'd never get hired.

Have you ever seen someone less skilled or experienced than you land jobs you would like to have?

The trick is to show hiring managers who you are. Thus, your personality needs to shine through, particularly when you're online.

I had a blog reader pick playful as one of her personality traits. Applying this to her brand, she showed a LinkedIn profile picture of her playing a video game guitar. Although it was a well-taken picture, it didn't fit into most people's definition of professional. That was OK, though, because as a creative marketing professional, she knew that playfulness is appreciated in her industry. In keeping with the "you/them" model of branding [Page 8], she aligned her message with both who she was and what a company would want. As a result, her dream company found her brand charming and snapped her up.

When I show my college audiences her picture and then tell her story, they love that they can be free to be who they are and not have to comply with someone else's definition of what professional means. Indeed, every decision you make in your career will come from these branding decisions you are making now. Don't let anyone tell you, "That's not professional." If you can back up your decisions with good research, you'll be fine!

Hal Thomas, an independent freelance designer in Savanna, GA, was hired based not just on his skills but also his dry humor. Hiring manager Sloan Kelly told me, "The most fascinating part of hiring Hal was that by the time he sat across from me at the interview, I already knew who he was." Sloan was able to envision what it would be like to work with Hal, and she liked him. Shouldn't that be your goal when looking for a job? Social media is the best way to demonstrate your personality! You can read—and hear—about Hal's remarkable job search in my blog interview here: http://careerenlightenment.com/hal-thomas-the-twitter-job-seeker

Exercise 3: Picking Your Personality Traits

Step 1: Brand associations

Answer the following four questions. They may seem irrelevant, but trust me, they're fun to answer and, if you take them seriously, they will give you great insight into your personality.

 Your personality traits influence your voice. Consider sharing this exercise with your career coach, resume writer, or LinkedIn profile writer, visit *http://liprofile.com*

Example: If you could be an animal, what would it be? Why?

Black bear, because they know the right time to take drastic action and the right time to be patient. Their power is in their ability to understand the situation at hand and then respond accordingly. Also, you don't mess with their cubs!

1) If you could be an animal, what would it be? Why?

_____

_____

2) If you could be a household appliance, what would it be? Why?

_____

3) If you could have a super power, what would it be? Why?

_____

4) If you could be a car, what kind would it be? Why?

_____

_____

Step 2: Find the pattern

Look back at your answers. Do you see any patterns? Do any of the following personality traits stand out to you?

Based on the previous exercise, and what you know about yourself, circle six to eight adjectives from below that best describe you. If these aren't enough, you can find 638 more on this MIT research page: *http://careerenlightenment.com/mit-attributes*

Dynamic	Adventurous	Accomplished
Creative	Savvy	Big (personality)
International	Energetic	Charming
Connected	Introverted	Formal
Self-assured	Accurate	Happy
Honest	Organized	Loving
Successful	Spirited	Political
Positive	Community-oriented	Risk-taking
Optimistic	Worldly	Sophisticated
Diplomatic	Modest	Colorful
Outgoing	Devoted	Funny
Extroverted	Humble	Healthy
Supportive	Religious	Motivating
Persuasive	Zen-like	Precise
Loyal	Trustworthy	Sassy
Adaptable	Enterprising	Spiritual
Convincing	Assertive	Conservative
Driven	Refined	Generous
Easygoing	Strategic	Intelligent
Wise	Inspiring	Passionate
Bright	Physically Fit	Pro-active
Dramatic	Enthusiastic	Shy
Quick-witted	Discerning	Striving
Flexible	Interested	Entrepreneurial
Methodical	Cheerful	Giving
Self-motivated	Bold	Inventive
Curious	Socially conscious	Picky
Likable	Dependable	Reliable
Ambitious	Ethical	Sincere
Quirky	Competitive	Visionary
Confident	Collaborative	

[Source: According to William Arruda, founder of 360Reach, http://www.reachcc. com/360reach, these are the main attributes that personal brands might have.]

Exercise 4: What's Your Freak Factor?

> ❝I used to bite my tongue and hold my breath
> Scared to rock the boat and make a mess
> So I sat quietly, agreed politely
> I guess that I forgot I had a choice
> I let you push me past the breaking point
> I stood for nothing, so I fell for everything❞
>
> —Katy Perry, Roar

You have a voice. Use it.

The job market is way too competitive now to blend in and comply. Companies are looking for people who are remarkable, unique, and invaluable to their goals.

Back in the 1960s and 70s, this wasn't the case. Guess what? We're not in the 60s and 70s anymore! You want to be the nail that sticks up or else you will be passed over.

Find Your Freak Factor

What's something you do in your life that is unconventional, even "freaky"? Maybe it's something you don't share with most people, and when you do, they raise their eyebrows in fascination. For me, people find it cool that I lived in Nepal for three years and I'm fluent in Tibetan. I have a friend who has pet snakes. What's yours?

_____

_____

_____

_____

_____

What's something you've always wanted to do in your life but haven't done? Maybe you've been too scared to do it or just haven't had the chance. If money or failure was not a concern, what would you do?

_____

_____

Your Strengths and Weaknesses

Peter Drucker, the great business thinker, said that by focusing on your weaknesses, "you'll have little chance of becoming even mediocre." But by focusing on your strengths, you can excel to a star performer.

In his well-known 2005 article, "Managing Oneself," Drucker puts it like this: "It takes far more energy and work to improve from incompetence to mediocrity than it takes to improve from first-rate performer to excellence." You can read his full article here:

http://careerenlightenment.com/peterdrucker

❝By focusing on your strengths, you can excel to a star performer.❞

The point: Focus on improving your strengths, and avoid situations where your weaknesses can pull you down.

To do this, you have to know your strengths and weaknesses.

_____

_____

_____

Exercise 5: Identify Your Strengths

Strengths

There are many ways to classify someone's strengths. Perhaps you've heard of some of these.

For the last 10 years or so, the Gallup organization has been studying people's strengths in a project called StrengthFinder 2.0. Using a unique battery of questions, they can tell you what your top five strengths are out of their list of 34. For example, here are mine: Intellection, Connectedness, Futuristic, and Restorative.

The StrengthFinder is about $24, but you can take a free version of the test by clicking on "Brief Strengths Test" in the middle of the page:

http://careerenlightenment.com/upenn-assessments

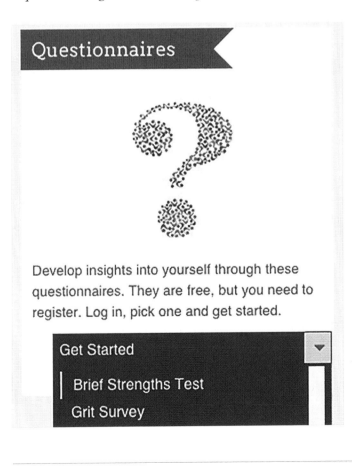

What are your five key strengths and what do they mean to you?

_____

_____

Skills

What relevant skills have you acquired throughout your life and career? What, would you say, are you really good at doing? Be specific and concrete.

_____

_____

What are some other ways of describing those skills?

_____

_____

What might be other applications of those skills (think unconventionally)?

_____

_____

Knowledge

What certifications or credentials do you possess?

_____

_____

What trainings have you been through?

_____

_____

What books have you read, or self-education have you enjoyed, that have most impacted the way you think?

_____

_____

Abilities

What are your innate abilities? What have you always been very good at?

Example: I'm really good at details. I can see small things and I'm compelled to fix them for the big win.

_____

_____

How do these innate abilities make you different from everyone else?

Example: attention to detail, meticulous, in compliance

_____

_____

Exercise 6: Identify Your Weaknesses

In order to avoid finding yourself in a situation that reveals your weaknesses, you have to know what they are first. Have you ever watched American Idol? Some people shouldn't be auditioning, yet there they are, and they believe they are good. Ouch. Try to be your own mirror.

Be honest with yourself. If you are, then you'll notice that you don't like doing certain things. Well, if you don't like doing it, chances are it's because you are a bit weak in that area. Though this isn't always the case, it's a good clue. For example, I've had a hard time handling a boss. I've been told I'm hard to manage. So I started my own business and I don't have a boss anymore.

Identify Your Weaknesses

Looking honestly at your life and career, what have you struggled with? What would you consider to be your weaknesses? You may have tried to improve in these areas , but no matter what you do, you're still aware of the deficiency. List these things here.

Tuning into your weaknesses helps you avoid wasting time pursuing jobs you would hate.

_____

_____

_____

_____

_____

Your Interests

In 1987, Ben Carson successfully performed a surgery that, for the first time, separated Siamese twins joined at the head. His feat is now considered a milestone in pediatric neurosurgery, a field where Carson is now regarded as a worldwide expert. But he almost didn't pass his job interview, at least according to the biographical movie, Gifted Hands.

With someone so clearly talented at what he does, what went wrong? Here's how the movie reenacts Ben's job interview.

Interviewer: Johns Hopkins accepts only two students a year. This year we have 125 applicants. So why should we take you?

Carson: Well, I have good grades and excellent recommendations.

Interviewer: As do all of our applicants.

Strike one. The interviewer was asking the question "What makes you different?" and Ben blew it. He answered with his qualifications rather than his personal brand. The interviewer is fast to point out this error. So he tries again…

Interviewer: You have confidence. That is good for a neurosurgeon. But tell me something, why did you decide to become a brain doctor?

Carson: The brain…it's a miracle. Do you believe in miracles? Not a lot of doctors do. There isn't a lot of faith among physicians. We study reports; it's all very tangible. But the fact is, there are so many things we just can't explain. I believe we are all capable of performing miracles, up here (points to head). We are blessed with astonishing gifts and skills. Look at Handel. I mean, how can he come up with The Messiah in only three weeks (pointing to head again). This is the key. The source of inspiration for unbelievable accomplishments.

Interviewer: You like classical music?

Carson: I love it.

Interviewer: I do too. I think we'll get on quite well together. (They shake hands and he gets his Hollywood ending.)

Let's review what went right:

- Carson expressed his deep interest in understanding the brain, and he brought in emotion and drive rather than mechanical qualifications.

- He took a risk about bringing his faith into the conversation. In this case, it didn't hurt him; it is who he is. In fact, Ben is a deeply religious man. If you are going to work with him, you'd better accept that part of him.

- In a seeming non-sequitur, the interviewer picked up on Carson's love of classical music. Why? **Because it's a similarity. And it is our similarities that bring us together.** Ben could not have anticipated this, not unless he had seen the interviewer's LinkedIn profile during his research (wink wink).

The way you articulate your interests during your job search may determine whether you get passed over—or get the job.

Exercise 7: Explore Your Interests

Answer these three questions. Vary your answers between indoor and outdoor actives, solitary and group actives, artistic or technical activities if you can. The more types of interests you can talk about, the more interesting you will be!

1) What would I do all day if I had the chance?

_____

_____

2) Why do I love doing these things?

_____

_____

3) Why is it worth spending my time on these activities?

_____

_____

Your Values

❝Until you make the unconscious conscious, it will direct your life and you will call it fate.❞

—Carl Jung

Why do we do anything? Because of the unique combination of values that drive our choices. A value might be adventure or status or truth. You make choices based on your unique combination of values, you set value priorities to match your beliefs and assumptions about the world, and these assumptions come from both who you are innately and your environment (read: life experiences).

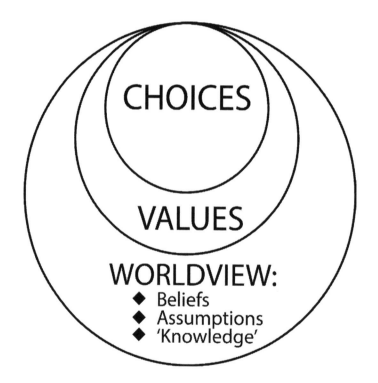

Gaining clarity on your own value system will help you:

Make better life and career choices.

- Feel more confident with who you are.

- Get motivated about your career direction.

Knowing what you value most in life can make decision-making very simple. For example, if you value family above all else, then you might decide not to accept any job that requires you to travel more than 30% of the time, no matter how much they pay you. If you value health above all else, then you might refuse to work for any company that sells unhealthy products, no matter how much they pay you.

At the core of every human being is a set of values that are unique. There may be other people applying for the same jobs who are just as qualified or skilled as you, but few have the same combination of values that you have. Knowing what this combination is will give you the confidence to make critical decisions about your life and career.

The confidence of knowing your life's unique combination of values can motivate you towards what ever it is you're trying to accomplish, like finding a job.

> When a reporter asked Michael Jordan how he scored so many 3-point shots, he replied, "I've missed more than 9000 shots in my career. I've lost almost 300 games. 26 times, I've been trusted to take the game winning shot and missed. I've failed over and over and over again in my life. And that is why I succeed." More than just winning, Jordan highly values learning, persistence, and passion. Tapping into your values will give you the strength you need to take more shots.

If you are interested in seeing a long list of values to help you with the following exercises, check out *http://careerenlightenment.com/values-list*

Values Elicitation Exercises

People are happy, motivated, and fulfilled when they live congruently with their personal values. This is what makes personal branding different than from branding. **A tube of toothpaste doesn't require that it feel good about the choices it's making and how it's representing itself on the shelf.**

Most people are unconscious about how their values affect their priorities. If you're not living your own values, whose values are you living?

By completing these assessments of your values, you can transform your values into conscious priorities, which will affect your personal brand. Insight into your top-priority values reveals why certain circumstances make you excited while others make you frustrated.

> **❝If you're not living your own values, whose values are you living?❞**

Complete the following exercises to better understand your personal values so that you can take charge of your brand—and ultimately give yourself the best chance of living the life you want.

Exercise 8: Finish the Sentences

Finish the sentence fragments below. Don't think too much about this. Just have fun and write down the first thing that comes to mind.

If I only had 24 hours to live, I would...

_____

_____

If I had a million dollars, the first thing I would do is...

_____

_____

People who know me think I'm...

_____

_____

Many people don't agree with me about...

_____

_____

Exercise 9: Whom Do You Admire Most?

Often, the people you admire most have had the most profound influence on your character. These people can be relatives, musicians, activists, or just people you have heard about. There are no limits to whom you can choose, except that they must have had an impact on your life and the way you see the world.

Often, people show their values by sacrificing something. When thinking about the values your person exemplifies, think about what he or she were willing to give up in order to accomplish what he or she accomplished.

Someone You Admire	Why You Admire Them	What Values They Exemplify

Exercise 10: What Are You the Most Proud of in Your Career?

Think back to a time in your career when you felt the most proud. In the space below, write about what happened and what role you played in that success. Please be as vivid in your retelling as possible. Write down what you saw, felt, and heard.

_____

_____

_____

_____

What is it about this event that compelled you to choose it over any other?

_____

_____

_____

_____

Using the list on the next page as a guide, what three values do you see in yourself in this experience? For example, in your memory, did you show perseverance and a drive for honesty and did you demand the best from yourself?

_____

_____

_____

_____

What makes you the best at what you do?

_____

_____

_____

_____

Exercise 11: Stack Rank These Values

Look through this list of values from Michael "Dr. Woody" Woodward. Circle the five that resonate with you the most. If you need a longer list of values, you can find one here: *http://careerenlightenment.com/values-list*

Remember, this is about value priority. You may love all of these values, but which ones do you love more? Yes, you have to pick just five.

Achievement	Freedom	Personal development
Advancement/promotion	Financial gain	Physical challenge
Adventure	Friendships	Pleasure
Affection (love and caring)	Growth	Power and authority
Arts	Having a family	Privacy
Challenging problems	Helping other people	Public service
Change and variety	Helping society	Purity
Close relationships	Honesty	Quality of what I take part in
Community	Independence	Quality relationships
Competence	Influencing others	Recognition (respect, status)
Competition	Inner harmony	Religion
Cooperation	Integrity	Reputation
Involvement	Intellectual status	Security
Country	Responsibility/accountability	Self-respect
Creativity	Job tranquility	Serenity
Decisiveness	Knowledge	Sophistication
Democracy	Leadership	Stability
Ecological awareness	Location	Status
Economic security	Loyalty	Supervising others
Effectiveness	Market position	Time freedom
Efficiency	Meaningful work	Truth
Ethical practice	Merit	Wealth
Excellence	Money	Wisdom
Excitement	Nature	Work under pressure
Fame	Being around honest people	Work with others
Fast living	Order	Working alone

What are your top five personal values?

Look back at the last four values eliciting exercises. Do you see any patterns or themes emerging? Is there something in common in all of your answers? Using the information from the earlier exercises, list here your top three driving values. These words should be the essence of who you are, values that will not change whether you are knitting at home or running an office. In addition, write them down and put them in a place you can see them every day.

 Consider sharing this exercise with your career coach, resume writer or LinkedIn profile writer. For more information, visit *http://liprofilecom*

1. _____

2. _____

3. _____

4. _____

5. _____

Your Values Must Be Unique

A word of caution. Most people share common values like family, belonging, or security. These are basic human drives and not value priorities unique to you. Having them doesn't differentiate you from most homo sapiens.

What I'm looking for from you is a personalized and prioritized list of values. The more you know which values you consider more important, the easier it will be for you to articulate your personal brand to a potential employer.

When you've come up with a value, put it through this four-part test from psychologist Dr. Michael "Woody" Woodward, author of The YOU Plan.

1. Am I really willing to pay, fight, or sacrifice to meet this value?

2. If yes, what would I be willing to pay, fight, or sacrifice for this particular value?

3. Do I truly live this value? (always, sometimes, never)

4. Where does this value come from? (family, faith, culture, education, life experience)

During a live training, I often have to push people to go deeper than just family or security. Usually, there's something beneath that. For example, you might say that you admire your mother. I'll ask you, "Why do you admire your mother?"

"Well, she sacrificed her free time in order to provide for her family, so family must be my value too."

"Why is family important to you?"

"Well, because I'd like to know they'll be there when I need them. "

"So if you got a job offer for 1 million dollars but you had to move away from your family for a year, would you take the job?"

If you say, "Yes" then I know your value isn't just family, but also something to do with being able to provide for them, maybe reliability or stability or wealth.

Push yourself to go deeper.

Your Mission and Vision

Mission and vision statements are used as a tool to encourage you to consciously reflect on who you are and where you are going with your life. As the Cheshire Cat says, "If you don't know where you're going, any road will get you there. "

If you are following Tom Peters' advice by becoming Brand You and running your career like a small business, then it's logical that you should also have a well-defined vision and mission statement, just like any business.

Your vision is where you are headed. How you get there is your mission statement.

Complete the next exercises to build these tools for yourself.

Exercise 12: Crafting Your Vision Statement

A vision statement is a statement of three or four sentences describing a desired future—not a predicted future—but one you want to see for yourself. Think of it as a big goal, from 30,000 feet up. It is the vision of how you want to lead your life.

Examples:

I am more physically fit, almost finished with my formal education, actively involved in two close personal relationships, worshipping and serving God regularly, having fun every day and making at least 75% as much money as now doing work that I love.

– Pastor Steven Poenitz

I am a change agent and leader for programs and organizations to bring about the value of each individual and live in a world where each person can contribute to society using their unique talents authentically.

– Susan Chritton, Personal Branding For Dummies

Close your eyes and picture yourself in the future. It may be a few months or years from today. See the person you are, what you are doing, who you are with, what you have accomplished, what is important to you, and how people relate to you. How does it feel to be you? Feel the person you are, your true self. Now, open your eyes and answer the following questions:

Three things I'd do if I won the lottery	1. 2. 3.
Issues or causes I deeply care about	1. 2. 3.
The two best moments of my past week	1. 2. 3.

My most important values	1.
	2.
	3.
Things I really enjoy doing	1.
	2.
	3.

Now you try. Thinking of who you are in your ideal future, write your vision statement in the space below. Keep it under 50 words. Take your time. The more thought you put into your vision statement, the better it will serve you in crafting a powerful mission statement.

My vision statement:

Exercise 13: Crafting Your Mission Statement

You mission statement explains how you will accomplish your vision.

Your personal mission statement is not a to-do list (although you will certainly create to-dos based on it). It should answer these three questions:

1. What is my life about (Purpose)?

2. What do I stand for (Values)?

3. What actions do I take to manifest my purpose and my values?

Examples:

> *To find happiness, fulfillment, and value in living, I will seek out and experience all of the pleasures and joys that life has to offer. My core values are not limitations restraining me on this hedonistic quest for fun. Rather, they provide a framework for identifying, pursuing, and achieving those pleasures that last the longest and are the most satisfying. The greatest joy of all is being worthy of the respect and admiration of family, friends, and business associates. (Ronnie Max Oldham, Australia)*

Here are some sample personal mission statement sentence templates to get you started (thanks to the University of Louisiana)

> *"To ... [what you want to achieve, do or become] ... so that ... [reasons why it is important]. I will do this by ... [specific behaviors or actions you can use to get there]."*

> *"I value ...[choose one to three values]... because ...[reasons why these values are important to you]. Accordingly, I will ...[what you can do to live by these values]."*

> *"To develop and cultivate the qualities of ...[two to three values/character traits]... that I admire in ...[an influential person in your life]... so that ...[why you want to develop these qualities]."*

> *"To live each day with ...[choose one to three values or principles]... so that ...[what living by these values will give you]. I will do this by ...[specific behaviors you will use to live by these values]."*

> *"To appreciate and enjoy ...[things you want to appreciate and enjoy more] by ...[what you can do to appreciate/enjoy these things]."*

> *"To treasure above all else ...[most important things to you] by ...[what you can do to live your priorities]."*

> *"To be known by ...[an important person/group]... as someone who is ...[qualities you*

want to have]...; by ...[some other person/group]... as someone who is ...[other qualities]...; ... "

Now you try. Keep it under 100 words. Take your time. The more thought you put into your mission statement, the better it will serve you in discovering career directions that you find fulfilling.

My mission statement:

_____

_____

_____

_____

THEM: Understanding Their Needs

Remember our discussion of the You|Them model back on page 8? Since then, this workbook has focused on You. Now we turn attention to the often-missing half of personal branding: Them.

Do you fully understand the needs of your target organization or even of the person likely to make a hiring decision about you?

Take this situation for instance. You just bought a yellow VW Bug. As soon as you drive it off the lot, you notice the same car everywhere! Hasn't something like this happened to you?

One of two things is going on. First, all of a sudden, thousands of people decided to buy the same car as you at the exact same time…or, more likely, something happened to your brain so that you are now paying more attention to this kind of car.

Obviously it was option two. The "something" that happened to your brain is called priming the reticular activating system (RAS). The RAS is just a small part of the brain but it serves an important function: it filters out unimportant information and filters in important information. Priming is how the RAS knows what is or isn't important. Usually there is some event that causes priming, like buying a car, reading an article about something, or dealing with issues or goals at work. Without this priming, our awareness would be completely overwhelmed by silly details or irrelevant sensory perceptions.

Hiring managers who are trying to hire a specific type of person to solve a specific need in their organization have primed their RAS to zero in on people who can fill that need. All others get ignored. This is great news for you, the job seeker. It means that if you understand their needs, you can address it in your online profiles, in your resume, and in your communications with the certainty of getting their attention. This also explains why so many job seekers get ignored from consideration; their application simply doesn't address the needs of the person making the decision.

So when I ask you to prepare a top ten list of target companies in a moment, it's not just because that's what career advisors are supposed to ask you. It's based on an understanding of the brain and how to get the attention of target people.

The steps below will show you how to easily build that list of names and then research their needs. In part two of this training, you will learn how to transfer this research into your profiles and communications so your message makes the biggest and best impression possible.

Exercise 14: Build Your Top 10 List of Companies

If you don't already know what companies you would LOVE to work for, this exercise will help you come up with that list. Remember that it is extremely important to be specific.

1) Start by browsing the various industries on LinkedIn. Follow this link to a page that has been hidden by LinkedIn: *http://careerenlightenment.com/industry-list* and select your preferred industry.

2) Next, filter down your list of companies by your preferences, such as company size or location.

3) Finally, search within these companies for contacts with roles you suspect would be in a position to hire you. For example, if you want a marketing job, find the VP of marketing. If you want a developer's job, find the director of product development.

Zoominfo.com is another great online resource for finding a good list. Not every industry is represented well on LinkedIn. So *Zoominfo.com* may be a better tool for you.

 To learn how, watch:
http://careerenlightenment.com/wb-top-10-companies

Write your results in the first column of the table on the next page.

Finding what your target organizations need

With ubiquitous access to the Internet, most employers expect candidates to know quite a bit about their company before applying. Research on your target company is therefore considered a baseline requirement. Fortunately, this research is easy and simply requires your time and your ability to organize the information in a useful way.

It's best to begin your research at a high level and work your way down. Start by examining your industry, work your way down to the ecosystem of companies (your company and their competitors), then drill down to issues with your company and even with an individual at the company whom you might wish to talk to.

 If you work with my team to write your LinkedIn profile, my writers need to know which companies you're targeting and what their needs are. Be sure to share this information during your intake process.

Leverage your social media skills by looking to these resources for your research:

Industry and Company Research

- *alltop.com* for human-curated news from the top blogs
- *search.twitter.com* for what's trending on Twitter
- LinkedIn Groups and Company Pages for trends and how they talk about themselves
- *news.google.com* for global, up-to-date news aggregation

To learn how, watch: *http://careerenlightenment.com/wb-company-needs*

People Research

- LinkedIn profiles of the people who work at your target companies
- Zoominfo to get the names of senior leaders
- Pipl, Spokeo, PeekYou, and other research tools
- Google their names using "quotation marks" around the name; if it's a common name, add some kind of identifier, like location, company, or job title
- Search.twitter.com to see if they're talking or being talked about

 To learn how, watch: *http://careerenlightenment.com/wb-people-needs*

Exercise 15: The Needs of Each Company You Are Targeting

Industry | Company | Job| Possible Decision Maker	Burning need or goal	How you can help (story)
1. Example: Keen Footwear	High shipping costs in global distribution due to operational inefficiency	Bring experience from AT&T where you saved them $2M by implementing LEAN methodology
2.		
3.		
4.		

After completing this table, are there any themes that emerge? If you could boil down the value you add to these companies to just a single offer, what would it be?

_____

_____

_____

_____

Understanding Keywords

Thanks to search engines, and by extension, to resume-crawling software that HR departments use to pre-filter candidates, using the right nouns can either get you a job or keep you in the unemployment line.

Because you are targeting specific jobs with specific companies, no one can give you a list. There are many tools to help you, but the best one comes directly from the industry or company you are targeting.

Exercise 16: Finding YOUR Keywords

Complete the following exercise to find your top ten list of keywords. This list will help you in writing your personal branding message and your online profiles.

 Be sure to share your top 10 keywords with your LinkedIn profile writer or resume writer so he or she can use them in your profile.

1. Use your brain first

In order to start your keyword list, just imagine that you're an HR recruiter looking for someone to fill an open position. What words would you type into Google to find someone to fill that opening? For example, if you're an HR recruiter looking for a museum curator, you might search the following words: preservation professional, collection management, exhibition development, or even history enthusiast.

Write out words that you think people would use to describe what you do:

_____

_____

_____

_____

2. Build your word cloud

This is what a word cloud looks like. It visually represents words from any body of text based on frequency. The more important words may appear more frequently.

Now it's time to build your own. Follow these steps:

1. Visit your favorite job board and look for a job opportunity that best represents what you want to do. For example, hop on over to indeed.com and type in your job title. Ignore the location for now. You're not actually applying.

2. Open a word processor or text editor and copy the entire job description there.

3. Do this for two more job descriptions. Use a different job board if you like. By the end of this step, you should have a text document with three different job descriptions for the same type of job all together.

4. Visit *http://www.onetonline.org/* and find the official description for your job. If the exact job title isn't there, just find one as close as possible and paste that at the bottom of the text document as well.

5. Finally, copy that entire document (3 jobs and 1 O*Net description) into your favorite word cloud generator. The ones I use are *wordle.net*, *tagxedo.com*, or *tagcrowd.com*. Choose Create, paste in your text, and voilà!

6. Analyze your word cloud and see if you can spot new keywords in the graphic. Write them down.

To learn how, watch: *http://careerenlightenment.com/wb-word-cloud*

Keywords versus, the art of the long-tail

One of the major limitations of using wordclouds is that they only provide you with one-word answers. If you separate "social" from "media" then you aren't full capturing the complete meaning of the phrase "social media". If you see "executive" popping out in a wordcloud, you might miss that this popular term actually should be "sales executive", something entirely different.

As a rule of thumb, avoid relying on single words as they will tend to be too generic or too competitive. A recruiter isn't going to type "sales person" in a LinkedIn search, but they might type, "Software Sales Rep".

The more you can qualify the phrase, the better off you will be. For example, use "hospitality sales manager" over the more generic "sales manager" when researching words. This will be particularly important for this next step on stack ranking your keywords.

3. Analyze with a keyword tool

Step 1: Log in to Google Adwords

Follow this link and sign in with your Google account:

https://adwords.google.com/KeywordPlanner

Step 2: Choose the Search Volume Tool

You'll pick the 2nd option for search volume that says, "Get search volume for a list of keywords". See screenshot below.

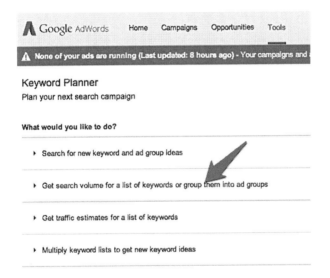

Step 3: Enter Your Words and Analyze

Copy and paste your list of words into the empty field. Then run the report. You'll want to pick the 2nd tab that says, "Keyword Ideas". See screenshot

In this example, the writer learns that Specialist is a much better choice of words getting 40,500 monthly searches versus Strategist, which only gets 8,100.

Your top ten keywords

Write down your top ten keywords and use them as much as possible when you write your profiles. Some people print these out and post them near their computer.

Tip: avoid using single words. Read the previous section called, "Keywords Versus Keyphrases" to understand why this is critical. This list will include job titles of various permutations, qualifying characteristics, the names of software you're specialized in, the names of techniques you're certified in etc.

1

2

3

4

5

6

7

8

9

10

Summing up Your Brand

If you would like to feel a sense of clarity and direction about your career, knowing your personal branding profile is essential. You've already done a lot of work clarifying YOU (values, passions, interests, etc). You've also researched THEM (your target industry and organizations) to make sure that you can offer a promise of value relevant to their needs. The next step is to put it all together and craft practical variations of your personal brand.

In the YOU/THEM model, this is where the YOU circle overlaps with the THEM circle. So when working at these next exercises, do your best to bring in the insights, themes, and patterns you identified earlier.

Exercise 17: Other Branding Decisions

Your brand gets communicated in everything you do and say. If you show up late, dress sloppily, or use curse words or a lot of slang, this affects your brand (how people see you and the promise you are making). Here are some other things to consider when making branding decisions (fill in your answers below each question):

What color(s) best represent you?

What behaviors exemplify your brand promise?

What clothing style most clearly communicates who you are?

Are you more casual or more formal, friendlier or more serious?

What's the one emotion you want people to feel when they remember your name?

Exercise 18: Your Personal Branding Profile

Reference the exercises you've completed so far in this workbook when filling out the following table. If you would like to print out this table for reference or to work on revisions, you can download a copy here: *http://careerenlightenment. com/personal-branding-table*

By collecting all aspects of your brand in one place, it will be easier for you to see any patterns, themes, or emotional qualities that might arise. Also, when it comes to making decisions about your online profiles, or even your career, you can use this table as a reference to see if you are truly congruent with it.

You'll be able to finish this table by the time you complete this first part of the workbook.

Download a copy here: *http://careerenlightenment.com/personal-branding-table*

My Personal Branding Profile	
Mission	
Vision	
Needs	
Values	
Strengths	
Personality Traits	
Other Branding	
Decisions	
Goals/objectives/ interest	
Keywords	
Target audience|	
Their needs	
Promise of Value	
Branding Statement	
Tag Line	

Exercise 19: Promise of Value

Your promise of value is a statement, for yourself, of how you plan to live your personal brand. This is the promise you make to other people of what you have to offer them, what value you can bring to them, what type of emotional experience they can expect from interacting with you.

Susan Critton, author of Personal Branding For Dummies, shares her promise of value:*I am known for my creativity, enthusiasm, and intelligence by serving eachclient with respect, giving them individual attention, and treating them with unconditional positive regard. I am an expert in my field and use my knowledge to help my clients and students excel. My clients appreciate my solid, grounded approach during times of transition and trust my guidance through the process.*

If you like formulas, you can try this one from Lida Critrön, from her book Reputation 360:

In order to be known for (your brand qualities):

I will hold myself out to others in this way (your behavior, actions, attitude):

And I will demonstrate authenticity in this way (how you will let people see that you are real, genuine):

I will know my brand promise is working when I see this (benefits to others, goals you want for yourself):

Now you try, keeping a copy of the personal branding table you've filled out on the previous page as reference. In the space below, using your own words, or using Critrön's formula, write your own promise of value.

_____

_____

_____

_____

_____

_____

This Is NOT an Elevator Speech

You may have an elevator speech ready to go. Maybe you deliver it at networking events or on the phone.

But what we are building here is not just another elevator speech. Here's why:

- An elevator speech answers the question "What do you do?" Although this is good to be able to articulate, it doesn't necessarily reflect your values and other branding considerations.

- An elevator speech is for someone else, and your personal branding statements are for yourself. Most elevator speeches sound like pitches.

- Your branding statements aren't limited to the 3-5 seconds typically available with an elevator speech because your branding statement isn't meant to be delivered orally.

- Most elevator pitches don't take into account your target audience's needs or keywords you need to pay attention to.

So when you go through the next series of exercises, I want you to ditch your elevator speech and start from scratch.

Exercise 20: Your Personal Branding Statement

Your personal branding statement is closely tied to your promise of value. In fact, your statement is simply the outward expression of that promise. By leveraging all of the work you've done so far in this section of the workbook, it's time for you to put all the pieces together into a single statement to encompass your brand.

To begin your thought process on what to include in your branding statement, answer the following four questions adapted from Be Sharp by Paula Asinof and Mina Brown:

1. What is at the core of who you are? Here, think about your passions and interests, when you feel "flow."

I know I am in my element when:

2. What is the knowledge, experience, or skills you hold that might interest your target? This is where your research comes in handy!

People recognize my expertise in:

3. What qualities do you possess that set you apart?

4. Other people comment on my ability to :

To give you a sense of what a personal branding statement might look like, William Arruda of Reach Personal Branding offers these examples: (from Personal Branding For Dummies by Susan Chritton, p. 121)

Sitting at the intersection of technology and business, I use my passion for communication to help IT professionals in Fortune 100 companies express themselves in ways that are understood by business people.

Through my intuition and genuine concern for – and interest in – others, I build long-lasting fruitful relationships with my team, my business partners, and my clients to drive consistent, recurring revenue for my company.

In working collaboratively with designers, I write witty, pithy, timely, and compelling copy for marketing materials for B-to-B companies.

If you need a more formulaic way to approach this, feel free to use this template, but it is by no means obligatory. Remember Mad Libs? Well, here's the personal branding version. Try it out!

I (verb) for (noun)_ who want to (value you offer) so they can (their outcome)_.

Here's one I wrote for a client:

I love to solve problems with global supply chain processes for Fortune 100 manufacturers who want to take advantage of the latest in Lead and Six Sigma so they can reduce costs and speed up time to market.

Now write your own (and remember to use a keyword or two):

Exercise 21: Your Tagline

Your tagline sums up your personal brand in a short pithy statement. It's something you can add to your business card or email signature. Taglines stick in people's heads. For example, I'm sure you can recall Nike's tagline: Just Do It!

Most taglines are usually fewer than 11 words and are clear enough so that anyone who reads it will instantly know what you do and how you can help them.

Susan Chritton also offers these wonderful examples:

Barbara Smith Accounting: Making Accounting Personal

Abigail Marks Marketing: Make Your Mark with Abigail Marks Marketing

Thomas Fuller, Personal Trainer: It's not just fitness...it's Personal

Now you try:

Exercise 22: Fill in the Rest

At this point, head on back to your Personal Branding Profile and fill in the rest of it. Or you can print up a new copy so you can keep it near you:

http://careerenlightenment.com/personal-branding-table

 Be sure to send a copy of this table, completed, to your LinkedIn profile writer or career coach so they can better understand who you are and write in your voice.

Congratulations, you have now discovered your personal brand. You've done more work than 99% of your competition. By the time you fill out your online profiles using your brand as a guide, you can expect to see quick results in your job search.

Part 2:

Polish Your Online Self

It's Time to Shine

Having read Part 1: Position Yourself, you are ready to move on to Part 2: Polish Your Online Self. In Part 2, you will learn how to translate all that personal branding stuff into concrete, powerful, online value statements. Because brevity is much harder than verbosity, you will start with the longest of the value statements, your LinkedIn Profile Summary, and end with the shortest, your LinkedIn Headline.

Polishing your online self means you will use your personal brand to build a job-attracting online reputation. You will build compelling profiles that are not only consistent, they will also be relevant to your target audience. Considering that your first impression will likely be online, this part is as important as getting dressed before a job interview.

One audience member emailed me after attending a talk where I taught these techniques. He told me that within a week of polishing his LinkedIn profile following advice you are about to learn, 17 people in his network approached him about his job search. He's now gainfully employed and credits the care he took when crafting his online messages. These seemingly small changes—this polishing effort—can have a very big impact on your life and career!

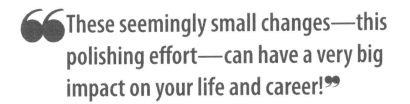

These seemingly small changes—this polishing effort—can have a very big impact on your life and career!

How Do You Know What Social Network to Use?

A common objection from many audiences I speak to is this: "I'm overwhelmed and all of this seems like so much time. How do I know what social network to focus on?"

In this part of the workbook, I'll tell you about the Daily Social Media 20-Minute Ritual. Basically, the time excuse doesn't work on me. You can't spend 20 minutes using social media? You probably spend twice that much on job boards!

In regards to knowing what social network to focus on, think of it like this: if you know that social media is a publishing tool, the first question a publisher like you should ask is "Where is my audience?"

- Facebook: over 1 billion users
- LinkedIn: over 330 million users
- Twitter: over 218 million users

If you want the fastest results and you are serious about finding meaningful work, you should find the time to be active on all three of these networks. This is your career, and these are tools to help you advance it. Can you really afford to be that picky?

However, if your ambition is somewhat overshadowed by your dislike of social networking, perhaps this can help.

- Use Facebook if you'd like to get referrals into unlisted jobs. (Who wouldn't?)

- Use Twitter if any of the companies you are looking at have a marketing department. (What company doesn't?)

- Use LinkedIn if your industry has recruiters. (What industry doesn't?)

Okay, did I make my point?

I wrote more on how to know if you know if you should be on LinkedIn here: http://careerenlightenment.com/linkedin-isnt

Your Social Media Profiles

When a hiring manager gets an email or an application from you, chances are he or she will look you up on LinkedIn or Google. How you look online will often be his or her first impression of you.

Sometimes hundreds of candidates apply for a single job, and most of them lead with their qualifications. However, according to some research widely available, hiring decisions are based on two other key factors: fit and motivation. Where a resume might limit you to showing just your qualifications, your social media profiles allow you to also show fit and motivation.

Just like my blog reader who brought playfulness and creativity into her online profiles to demonstrate fit, you too can find ways to be yourself while writing in this section. Step out of the old resume mindset and into an advertising mindset. When Coke advertises, they are infusing all kinds of emotional qualities onto a drink that is functionally the same as its competition, Pepsi. If they just stuck with function in their message, no one would buy it. A sweet fizzy drink with caffeine, oh yay, vs. thirst quenching, satisfying, and fun.

The same holds true of your online messages. If you just stick with what you can do, your experience and skills, it's hard for hiring recruiters to know why they should choose you.

At first, during career coaching calls, I would ask clients to tell me what makes them the best at what they do. New clients would invariably say, "I'm good with people" or "I have a strong work ethic." If you've gone to any job search groups in your area, you'll know everyone says this kind of thing. The mistake is that these adjectives all relate to job function, not to who you are. By leveraging the personal branding work, you can start to really infuse your answer to the question "what makes you the best" with your unique personality.

After some coaching, clients will start to say more exciting things like "I wake up to create something new, it's in my genes" or "some people think accounts payable is dull work, but I love building trusting relationships with our suppliers. It's the part of business that we have the most control over with the biggest effect to the bottom line, and that excites me."

Follow the exercises below to ensure that your first impression online will make you unforgettable.

Exercise 23: Writing Your LinkedIn Profile Summary

First, answer these four questions. Then, combine your answers into your LinkedIn profile summary. Remember to use at least two of your keywords.

1. Begin with an action plan statement that describes who you are, not just a job title.

"I'm an entry-level marketing professional specializing in digital media."

_____

_____

2. Add a one-sentence statement about what it is you do in the context of a problem you solve.

"When old marketing tactics stop working, I provide fresh ideas and a modern perspective that appeal to a younger audience."

_____

_____

3. Give a statement about what makes you the best at what you do, naming an accomplishment.

"As the author of Job Searching with Social Media For Dummies, I've helped thousands of job seekers demystify social media, make great connections, and get hired."

_____

_____

4. What are you looking for exactly? Be specific.

"If you're looking for a person to fill a challenging position in international marketing, advertising, or business development, please feel free to contact me.

_____

_____

To learn how, watch: *http://careerenlightenment.com/wb-4-steps*

Now take what you wrote in the previous four steps and put them all together in a way that is easy to read and flows well. Please underline your keywords when you're done.

_____

_____

_____

 This four-part framework is great if you are writing your LinkedIn profile yourself and you need to get a high-quality message posted quickly. If you are looking for more, my trained LinkedIn profile writers are able to expand your personal branding message for an online audience with over 12 different LinkedIn profile summary models. Be sure to share what you've done so far during the intake process.

Don't have a coach or writer? To learn about my LinkedIn profile writing services, visit *http://liprofile.com*

Discussion

1. Read the case study in the next section. What would you change about your profile summary based on that?

_____

_____

LinkedIn Summary Case Study

I received the following email from a blog reader asking for advice with her LinkedIn profile summary. She did a great job so far, and so I thought I'd let you listen in to my reply.

Dear Joshua, my name is AM and I am an aspiring marketing professional within the fashion industry. I recently did your 4-Step Tool for writing my LinkedIn Profile Summary. It was such a great exercise because my LinkedIn Summary is super long.

Since I am going through a re-adjustment of my personal branding, I came up with the following summary (below), but I am not sure whether it is good enough to be publish on LinkedIn:

I am an aspiring and driven marketing professional, specializing in strategic partnerships for artistic fashion brands. I have assisted with a combination of over 30 New York Fashion Week runway shows and presentations for the Essie Sponsorship. In addition to this, I am a blogger who enjoys writing about the bridge between art and fashion. I also like to inspire and motivate young people to pursue their dreams.

If you need assistance with fashion week, marketing, or blogging services for your company, please feel free to contact me.

I am struggling with "the problem I solve" part. Being a recent graduate, how do you find what the problem you can solve is? I know I like to do blogging (a form of content marketing) and I would love to possibly do it for other businesses if I could.

Thanks,

AM

AM, you've done a great job so far, certainly much better than the average summary statement and one that will still be effective. So this advice is just a matter of making some small changes. Here is the structure of what you currently have.

Sentence 1: Who you are (a marketing professional).

Sentence 2 and 3: What makes you the best (your experience at Fashion Week and interest in blogging).

Sentence 5: Call to action (contact me).

As you pointed out, you're missing the part where you mention the problem you solve. Here are some ways you can improve your statement.

1. Drop the "aspiring." You are who you say you are. And if you are going to be a marketing professional, than just be "a marketing professional." To say aspiring, I feel, puts yourself down.

2. Your mention about Fashion Week is great. I feel that there is more to the story, more you did there. Was this experience an unusual one for someone with your level of experience or your situation? What was the result? What did you love about it? For example, you might add, "I was excited to learn that I was the first intern to handle this much responsibility. All of the brands I worked with told me they enjoyed the experience."

3. You're right. You haven't quite put your finger on their problem or goal. I think your answer can be found in understanding why a company would want to blog. Here are some reasons I can think of:

A.   To create buzz

B.   To build a community

C.   To promote a product or event

D.   To improve search engine results

E.   To build their brand's thought leadership

Therefore, you can mention how you help fashion companies accomplish these things through your unique skills and interests. For example, "I love creating buzz around brands through publishing blog posts and articles. Writing about fashion and promoting trends has been something I've done since my junior year. If you're trying to get your fashion brand talked about by more people, then this is something I'd love to help with."

4. You can punch up your call to action a bit, again by tapping into your understanding of their needs and the benefits of what you offer. For example, "If you want your next Fashion Week to be the talk of the town, let me come up with a winning blogging plan for you. Email me at xyz@gmail.com."

5. You didn't mention this, but I noticed on your profile that you don't have multi-media elements uploaded. This is a missed opportunity to share pictures of you in action during Fashion Week or to link to some of the blog posts you've done. Use your profile to demonstrate the value you bring to them, not just what you've done in the past.

Exercise 24: Writing Your LinkedIn Professional Headline

You have 120 characters to communicate who you are and your value to an organization. Make sure you include your job title, and then explain how you help an organization solve a problem. Be sure to use at least one keyword. Feel free to tap into your personal branding tag line for inspiration. Think of your Headline as the shortened version of your Profile Summary.

- Recruiting high-impact candidates to great biomedical companies | Contract Recruiter

- Helping advisors build retirement plan sales through strategic marketing, communication, and education | VP Marketing

Now you try: (make sure it's not longer than 120 characters!)

_____

_____

 Although the shortest part of your profile, your Headline is the hardest to write. And it's particularly hard to write it for yourself, which is why many people chose to work with a coach or writer. Don't have a coach or writer? Check out my LinkedIn profile-writing services, here _http://liprofile.com_

Discussion

How would your headline change in order to:

1. Create Buzz

2. Build community

3. Promote a product or event

4. Improve search engine rankings

5. Build thought leadership

_____

_____

_____

Exercise 25: Writing Your Facebook Bio

On Facebook, you will have less space than on LinkedIn to describe who you are, and you want your statement to have fun, personal elements as well. Unlike LinkedIn, your connections on Facebook expect to see more of your personality. It would seem strange if you were all buttoned up on Facebook. Think of this as the happy hour party with colleagues after work. You're not in the office anymore, so you can reveal a little bit more about yourself.

Keep in mind as well that your Facebook network is a referral network. Your friends and family will be the ones passing on your information to companies. It's not like you'll be applying for jobs using Facebook. Recruiters probably won't be running keyword searches on Facebook looking for your unique set of skills. The 18 million jobs that Americans have found on this network all came because the people closest to them in their network cared about them and referred them into positions. That closeness can't be faked.

On Facebook, be who you are. Your friends and family love you for who you are. So never sacrifice your personality. Thankfully, you've already figured out what personality traits you want to communicate, from your work in Part 1.

Use the following three-step process to come up with a Facebook bio that tells the world what you do, why you do it, and who you are.

1. Answer the question: "What do you do?"

"I'm a sales engineer specializing in deploying software as a service application for large teams."

_____

2. Answer the question: "Why do you love doing what you do?"

"I believe cloud computing is our future and love to share what I know of the world's most powerful software solutions for big business impact."

_____

3. Reveal something fun and personal about who you are.

"When I'm not in the clouds, I love surfing with my 12-year-old and helping my wife tend our square-foot garden so we can enjoy fresh organic veggies."

_____

Now put it all together in a short statement that flows well; remember to use at least one keyword:

_____

Exercise 26: Writing Your Twitter Bio

You have 160 characters to express your personal brand on Twitter. Try this framework for filling out your Twitter bio. Remember, on Twitter, brevity is key. Forget complete sentences. Have fun. Show personality.

1. Who are you?

a. Use this space to write a 1-2 sentence answer:

ex. *"I really love raising money for causes, and building a community of like-minded people for events. People say I'm the queen of fund raising."*

b. Circle the three most important words from above and write them down here:

ex. *"Fund Raising Princess"*

_____

_____

2. Why you are the best at what you do?

a. Use this space to write 1-2 sentence answer:

ex. *"I feel strongly that people who can't afford treatment for their pets have a lower chance of survival. This drive me to ask the right people in the right way for money to save lives."*

b. Circle the six most important words and write them down here:

"when charming donors means saving lives"

_____

_____

3. Name a big win

a. Use this space to write 1-2 sentence answer:

ex. "I led an effort which raised $10,000 in just three months to save thousands of stray dogs."

b. Circle the ten most important words and write them down here:

"My Save the Dogs campaign raised $10k in 3 mo."

_____

_____

4. What do you want?

a. Use this space to write 1-2 sentence answer:

ex. "I want to make a positive difference for your organization or non-profit, whatever that mission might be."

b. Circle the five most important words and write them down here:

"making a difference for your non-profit"

_____

_____

Now put it all together, and this time pay close attention to character count: (make sure it's not longer than 160 characters!)

_____

_____

_____

_____

Now Upload Your Work to Your Profiles

Once you've written down your work here, now go online and type them into your profiles. You can feel confident that what you are writing about yourself is not just congruent with who you are, but that it also addresses the needs of your target jobs. Because you spent the time to figure out your personal positioning first, your online statements will be more consistent with each other.

Take a few moments now to upload your work. If you don't know how or where to put these elements, you can find technical support from the help section of each network or from grovo.com.

Here's what you've done so far:

- LinkedIn Summary
- LinkedIn Headline
- Facebook Bio
- Twitter Bio

So go ahead, login and upload your new, polished descriptions. I'll wait…

Advanced Profile Modifications

You now have a profile that works. Your messaging is consistent and powerful. Now you'll learn about the small modifications necessary to make your profile shine. After all, these days just having a profile isn't good enough. You have to have an AMAZING profile! Here's how.

The best way to work with this level of detail is with a checklist. Take a look at the checklists in the next section. Tick off what you already have completed, and put the rest in your to-do list. Many of the suggestions take just a few seconds, but they will make a huge impact on your hire-ability.

Note: The point of this exercise is to take advantage of those minor profile tweaks. Individually, they may seem small. But when combined, people who do this see better results from their social networking.

Advanced LinkedIn Profile Settings Checklist

Your LinkedIn profile will likely become the center of your entire professional personal brand. It will be your first impression. It will be your communications hub. It might even be your job application.

So don't ignore it or avoid it. If you're not making improvements to your profile on a regular interval, then you're not playing the game. Recruiters and employers have been using LinkedIn for many years, even though it might be new to you. With one look, they'll know how much effort you've put into making it look good which will reflect directly on your job prospects.

If you've ever felt apologetic for the state of your profile, now is the time to remove that blight from your life and make it shine.

Exercise 27: Audit Your LinkedIn Profile

In order to help you quickly find out if your LinkedIn profile is up to par, I've developed a quick grading tool which you can use right now. So let's see if your LinkedIn profile will get a 100% grade.

1. Visit: *http://profilegrade.com*

2. Connect your LinkedIn profile to run the app

3. Write down your grade and follow any instructions you're given

My Profile Grade is _____ %

To help you organize your profile improvement plan, I've listed here all of the major elements of your profile that need to be considered.

Open your LinkedIn profile and compare what you have with the items on this audit list. Check the box next to the audit item you've already completed. If an item is not yet completed, write down the day you plan to complete it.

If you get stuck on how to make these changes, get in the habit of looking up how to do something online. For example, if you don't know how to customize your links, simply search Youtube or Grovo for the feature you are trying to use. LinkedIn's help page also offers clear instructions: http://help.linkedin.com.

Please complete the table below, use an X for items already completed, otherwise, write down the date you plan to complete it.

For Groups

If you're learning in a group, find a partner and audit each other's profiles. Spend about five minutes per person.

Audit	Description	Est. Date of Completion
Vanity URL	Change the link to your public profile to include your name.	_____
Customize Links	Rename your outgoing links to include your other profiles, with custom names.	_____
Add Skills	Be sure to add skills, certifications, and/ or publications.	_____
Get Endorsed	Start endorsing people in your network; they will endorse your skills back. Try to get at least 50 endorsements on three of your top skills.	_____
Keywords	Include your best keywords in these five locations.	_____
Get to 500+ Connections	Size matters. (Did I just say that?)	
Get to 20 Recommendations	The more the better. You can't have too many. Every position you've held in the past should have at least five.	_____
Contact Settings	Change your Contact Settings so people know what you are open to, i.e., employment opportunities.	_____
Add Interests	Include interests so people can find commonalities with you.	_____
Location	Recruiters search on location; be sure you are specific and include the zip code of where you want to work, not necessarily where you live now.	_____
Have a current job	If possible, have a current position showing; it could be volunteer work or your own consulting business.	_____
Upload multi-media	If you have images, video, or slides that relate to your past experiences, upload them to your profile.	_____
Fill in the extra sections	Even if you are 100% complete, you can still add more info, like your project, publications and certifications.	_____

Exercise 28: Keyword-Optimize Your LinkedIn Profile

Recruiters use both LinkedIn and Google to search for candidates based on location and keyword. If they search on LinkedIn, search results will show up based on your degree of separation from them. If they use Google to search, results will show up based on the appearance of those keywords in certain key areas, considered by Google as more relevant. Follow these steps to increase your chances of ranking your LinkedIn profile.

Part 1: What Other People Do About Keywords or Phrases

Log in to LinkedIn and run a people search for your industry or role. Fill out the chart below to get a sense of how others are using keywords or phrases:

LI Profile	Word/ Phrase 1	Word/ Phrase 2	Word/ Phrase 3	Word/ Phrase 4	Word/ Phrase 5

Part 2: Optimize Your Own Profile Based on Keywords or Phrases

Look back at your list of top 10 keywords and compare them with what you found out from your competition in part 1. Now complete the following five exercises to better infuse these words for yourself.

1) Write Your Headline Before Keywords

_____

_____

Now, add 1-2 Keywords and rewrite your headline here:

_____

_____

2) Write Your Summary Before Keywords

_____

_____

_____

_____

Now, rewrite your summary adding 3-4 new keywords or phrases

_____

_____

_____

_____

3) Skills

Add your top 10 keywords to your Skills section. Write them down here.

4) Current experience title

What's your current job title?

_____

_____

Now add a keyword to that title and rewrite it here:

_____

_____

5) Current experience description

What's your current description of your experience?

_____

_____

_____

_____

Now re-write it infusing 3-4 of your keywords into it naturally:

_____

_____

_____

Note on keyword stuffing: Don't do it. It's ugly. It turns employers off. Write naturally and simply, and sparingly include the occasional keyword. This is not a system worth gaming. What matters more than keywords is the degree of separation you have with the person searching. Read the next section on how to include more of the right people in your network.

Getting to 500+ Connections

The larger your network, the more credibility you will be perceived as having and you'll show up in search results more frequently. This may seem juvenile and you may not agree with the practice or you may think it's morally wrong. (or maybe you read a blog post about how bad it is to be so cavalier with you LinkedIn connections). Just remember that you're using LinkedIn of one very specific goal: to find a job. In other words, the larger your network, the faster you'll find work. So drop any advice that is holding you back from having a large network. It's just hurting you.

LinkedIn is a tool to help you with your career. So keep an open mind and understand that having a large network is one of the highest predictors of getting found by recruiters. Period. No question about this. People with small, sub 500 networks, simple are not using this tool to it's fullest potential.

Luckily, the connection process is not very difficult. And while LinkedIn's original (and yet to be updated) policy is to make sure you are adding people to your network you know, their new features making it easier to add new people telegraph a very different message. Let's face it, LinkedIn want's to make it as easy as possible for you to have a large network…because that improves their shareholder value.

As a general policy, you should regularly take steps to grow your network. Here are some tips:

- Add everyone you've ever met in person and continue to do so immediately after you've meet someone new.

- Import your entire contacts list from your email client and connect with anyone who has a profile.

- Add ex-coworkers and alumni; use LinkedIn's alumni tool: *http://linkedin.com/alumni*

- Add group members you admire.

- Add recruiters; they never say no.

- Add LinkedIn Open Networkers or "LIONS", do a search for them in People Search; they also never say no.

Exercise 29: Add Recruiters to Your Network

The more recruiters you have in your network, the more likely it is you'll show up on the first page of search results for someone hiring for an open position.

Run an advanced people search with these steps.

1. Navigate to LinkedIn's advanced people search page

2. Use "Recruiter" as the keyword

3. Change the industry to the one you want to find a job in

4. Adjust the location to the place you want to work

5. Click Search and note how many recruiters appear on the results page

List five recruiters that you found in your industry:

1. _____

2. _____

3. _____

4. _____

5. _____

Now go ahead and invite all of them to connect with you.

Note: If you aren't getting many results in your search, follow these steps:

1. Remove the location filter and see if this improves things.

2. Join three industry relevant groups; then try again.

3. Join three groups where recruiters hang out (think professional association for recruiters); then try again.

To learn how, watch: *http://careerenlightenment.com/wb-add-recruiters*

Filling in Your Work Experience in LinkedIn

Unlike a resume where you might bullet-point each of your major accomplishments at each past position, on LinkedIn, a simple story is often good enough. Keep in mind that LinkedIn is not an online resume but rather a tool to inspire someone to contact you. Give recruiters and hiring managers just enough information so they can see your value. The best method for doing this effectively is by using the Problem/Action/Result (PAR) technique or statement.

The language of business is numbers. If you want to catch the attention of a business person, use numbers.

- How much?
- How many?
- When did you do it?
- How long did it take?
- How much time did you save?

- How much money did you save?
- How many people were involved?
- How many sales did you make?
- In what amount of time?
- What was your contribution to the company's bottom line?

Once you have their attention, you need to back up your statement with credible, verifiable results to prove that you are capable of doing what you say you can do. Use accomplishment statements (PAR statements – see below) in the body of your resume to demonstrate your capabilities.

Don't just state responsibilities. Give specific examples of how your actions have helped previous employers make or save money. For example, every office manager could put on his or her resume that he or she "organized and monitored office staff." Big deal. Nothing in that statement would be enough to get you an interview. Just think of what might happen if, instead, you put down something like this: "interviewed, hired, and trained 6 staff members to meet the needs of a fast-growing office environment." I can tell you what happened, because one of my clients put that on her resume and got several interviews because of it.

I recommend the PARS methodology to help you quantify your results and stand out from the competition.

Here's how to write your own PAR statements:

1. First, identify a specific PROBLEM (or situation or need) you worked on in a prior job or career position. Simply describe the need or the project you worked on. What was happening that needed your attention? Why was it important to your company? What would have happened if you'd done nothing? Whenever possible, use numbers to define the scope of the situation. Write two or three bullet points to identify the condition you encountered.

2. Second, describe the ACTIVITY or ACTION you took. What did you do to address the problem? List steps you took. Identify tools or processes you used. Don't worry about being too detailed here. Remember, this step is just for you. It doesn't go on your resume. In a few bullet points, describe the activity or action you took.

3. Third, describe the RESULTS that came about from your actions. What happened? Be sure to use quantifiable results. How much money did you make or save? How many people were involved? How much time was saved? How did you reduce waste or increase efficiencies? One or two bullet points ought to do it.

4. Finally, write a STATEMENT that shows the impact of the action you took. Write one or two sentences that pull together the 5-9 bullet points in the first three steps. These two sentences should bring all of your points together in a concise statement. A simple format for this is: "did what," "for whom," "resulting in…" Be sure to use numbers to show how the results were measured. This is important because managers use numbers to measure the success or failure of just about ANY business activity. When you quantify your results, you are speaking their language, and that is more likely to lead to an interview for you! Numbers make the accomplishment "pop" off the page. They allow you to stand out among the competition.

When people hire me to write their LinkedIn profile, I recommend coming up with 3-4 PARs for each key accomplishment area in the Experience Section. Use examples of different times, jobs, and situations to show a variety from your work history.

Here are some sample PAR statements to use as models, (thanks to career coach Sean Harry):

I project-managed the refurbishing and implementation of 2 wafer polishers working in a high-stress environment. Working with different departments to manage this project and understanding when to be direct and confrontational was key to finishing this project, which resulted in a savings of $300,000 and increasing polishing capacity by 15%.

Provided assistance for 200+ Japanese students during their English and American Culture and Business program at Portland State University.

Wrote, edited, and consolidated 150 pages of procedures down to 23 pages. Worked closely with operators to update and document every step of the operating procedure in the polishing department.

Designed a new online application and database to unify three separate admissions systems / databases when offices merged in 2007, allowing team to process applications 30% faster.

Streamlined admission process, which allowed office to process 400 applications in 2007 and over 500 applications in 2008 and 2009.

Developed the infrastructure needed to manage unique admissions requirements of each of our five graduate business programs, leading to increased matriculation rate of 12%.

Implementation of graduate program advising model of recruitment where I advised over 300 potential applicants annually resulting in 80% of those advised matriculating into one of our five programs.

Led team that provided infrastructure for over 35 info sessions annually, orientation for 250 students annually, and 2 separate graduate hooding ceremonies annually.

Exercise 30: Write Your First PAR Statement

Start off with just one PAR statement for your most recent role. Once you get the hang of this, apply it to all of your important experiences and add them to your LinkedIn profile.

Answer the questions below.

1. Pick a job you had?

What Problem did you solve?

What Action did you take?

What were the Results?

Write your full PAR statement here:

2. Pick another job you had?

P.

A.

R.

Statement:

3. Pick another job you had?

P.

A.

R.

Statement:

Keep going! You're on a roll!!

Optimizing Your Facebook Profile

Of the 18 million jobs that Americans found through Facebook, most of them came through referrals. After all, your Facebook network probably consists of your closest friends and family, the very people most likely to refer you to jobs.

Now, with Facebook's Graph Search, more and more recruiters are using Facebook to search out candidates. Those people who have filled out their work and education sections and made them public will show up on search results. This function is very much like LinkedIn. Therefore, it's imperative that you fill out your Facebook profile as completely as possible, making each section public.

If your work and experience sections match your LinkedIn profile, and if your personality comes through and shows a good fit, you may start getting random messages from employers via Facebook.

There are four parts to optimizing your Facebook profile:

1. Clean up past posts.

2. Limit/open up privacy and security settings strategically.

3. Allow parts of your About Me page to be public, including uploading good profile photos.

4. Post publicly to your wall at least once a week.

We'll talk about each one in the following sections.

Exercise 31: Clean up Past Posts

By the time my daughter turns 18, she'll have over eight years of Facebook posts out there in the wild webs. I'm fairly sure she hasn't read this workbook. I'm also sure she hasn't always paid much attention to the Audience setting on her posts. To be fair, I sometimes forget to check this too. Which means she's at a very high risk of having something on Facebook potentially damaging to her career.

So it's important that when you start your job search, you run a quick audit of your past Facebook posts and clean them up. Don't worry. It's a very simple process that doesn't require much time.

Visit http://simplewa.sh

1. Sign in by clicking the Facebook button

2. The tool will tell you what posts contain potentially undesirable words. You'll be able to see photos you've been tagged on for review

3. Clean a post either by deleting it or changing the audience to Me Only or Friends Only

Discussion

What posts do you need to clean up after your review?

_____

_____

What else can you do to feel more confident about what other people might see on your Facebook timeline?

_____

_____

If it's a train wreck: If you run an audit and you look and talk like a drunken sailor with five half-naked wives marooned on a desert island with nothing to eat but meatball grinders and twinkies, you can drop the a-bomb of profile clean up. Simply go to your Privacy and Settings, click on Who Can See My Stuff and click Limit Past Posts (see screenshot).

Exercise 32: Update Your Facebook Privacy Settings

Many Facebook users fail to spend any meaningful time understanding their privacy and security settings. Spend 30 minutes in your Facebook's settings area and really understand what each privacy and security setting does. I'm sure you didn't have professional networking in mind when you first set up your Facebook account, so now's the time to revisit your profile and make some changes!

1. Click the padlock icon for your security and privacy shortcuts;

2. Click on See More Settings for the full list of options.

3. Evaluate your settings in the following categories:

- Who can see my stuff

- Who can contact me

- Who can look me up

- Who can add things to my timeline

- Who can see things on my timeline

- How to manage tags

- Blocking

When choosing any of these settings, you may encounter one of the following privacy levels:

- **Everyone**: Content you deem safe for everyone is indexed by Google and appears on your public profile (so hiring managers can see it). I always set my bio and links to be viewed by Everyone because they're a part of my personal brand.

- **Friends and Networks**: This setting is for content that can be seen by second-degree connections and anyone who belongs to the same networks you do. (A network can include a school or a company.)

- **Friends of Friends**: Any content marked with this label can be seen by second-degree connections.

- **Friends Only**: Only your first-degree connections can view content with this label.

- **Friends except Acquaintances**: excludes any friends you've categorized as an acquaintance.

- **Myself only**: Self-explanatory!

- **Custom**: You can define what this means for each setting.

Discussion

After spending some time looking through your privacy settings, list what you discovered that was new or surprising about the kinds of controls you can have?

_____

_____

Now that you understand the control you have over your privacy, what will you keep public and what would you keep private? Who would you allow to post on your wall without your approval? Will these settings change for you after you've found a job? Why or why not?

_____

_____

_____

Editing Your Profile for Hiring Managers

Hiring managers can actually learn more about you if you spend the time to fill in your About You section and set its visibility to Public. There are tools for recruiters which use Facebook's profile information to suggest candidates in search results. The more your profile is filled out, the more chance you have of getting contacted by a recruiter.

Your profile info also helps Facebook find new people to suggest for your network. The more accurate your profile, the more accurate Facebook's suggestions are for recommended connections.

Here are the sections you should update for your job search.

Your profile photo

Your photo is attached to almost everything you do and is considered basic information in your privacy settings. The reason is that Facebook is—first and foremost—a visual platform.

If you're actively seeking employment, use your LinkedIn photo, or a professional photo, as your Facebook profile image. Unless you're interviewing for a hostess position at a nightclub (and maybe even then), you want your first impression on Facebook to be as professional as possible.

Your About You Section

When you click on the Update Info button at the top of your Timeline next to your name and look to the right of the page that appears, you find a box called About You that's just waiting to be filled with information about you. The About You section communicates who you are professionally and what makes you unique. Set the text you enter in this section to appear publicly. This may be the only information a hiring manager reads about you on Facebook.

If you want to add a little bit more personality or personal information as well, lead with a professional statement of who you are and then conclude with a more personal statement, perhaps mentioning some interests or hobbies.

Your Education and Work

Be sure you completely fill out your education and work history so that it matches your resume. Hiring managers are looking for inconsistencies (after all, some people lie on their resumes), so if they see that you're consistent with your resume in several places, they're more likely to respect you. Set these sections to be viewed publicly.

Your Philosophy

I don't recommend that you fill in your religious or political views in this section. However, sharing who inspires you and what your favorite quotes are can be powerful. Spend time thinking about your role models and any quotes that stick with you.

All the Other Profile Settings

Your Facebook profile also allows you to enter information about the types of music, books, movies, and TV shows you like, as well as your favorite sports teams, activities, and other interests. Don't be afraid to fill in this information. Sharing it helps round out your personality in the eyes of a hiring manager. Just keep in mind that your selections should be appropriate; use the "Would I talk about it in the office?" test to be sure. Revisit these parts of your profile periodically with your career in mind.

Exercise 33: Update Your Facebook About Me Section

Using the previous section as a guide, make those important changes to your Facebook About Me Section now.

Log into Facebook and click on your name in the top navigation.

1. Click on Update Info to access your profile information.

2. Fill out as much as you can and set each section to Public. The only sections to keep private, in my humble opinion, are religious views and political views.

Discussion

Was it easier filling out your Facebook About Me section after having completed Part 1 on Personal branding? Why or why not?

_____

_____

List the parts of your Facebook About Me section that you felt uncomfortable setting to Public?

_____

_____

How would you advise your friends to complete their About Me sections?

_____

_____

Exercise 34: Practice Changing Audiences

Most people set their default audience to Public and then never change it. Remember that Facebook is a publishing medium and a publisher always thinks about his or her audience.

Get in the habit of checking your audience for each post. Let's practice now.

1. Log into Facebook and come up a message you feel can be make Public, something a potential employer wouldn't mind reading.

Write your message for Public here:

_____

_____

2. Find the Audience button and set it to Public (see screenshot); then post it.

3. Next come up a message that you feel is just for your friends. An example might be a post about food, or your spouse/partner, or a picture of your beer (which I'm sure you're drinking while reading this great book!).

Write your message to Friends Only here:

_____

_____

4. Set that update to the Friends audience, then post it.

Discussion

How does this experience posting for two different audiences change how you will interact with Facebook in the future?

_____

_____

Will you update your default audience or keep it to Public? Why?

_____

_____

What types of posts absolutely must never be set to Public?

_____

_____

What kinds of posts might be a good idea to set as Public?

_____

_____

Exercise 35: See What Other People See

Now that you've completed the last four exercises, it's time to check out your progress. What will a hiring manager actually see when they check you out on Facebook?

To find out change your View As settings to see what your profile looks like from the perspective of someone not in your network. This is the view a potential hiring manager might have of you.

Watch this video to learn how to change your View, and set it to public.

 http://careerenlightenment.com/wb-facebook-view

Discussion

If you were meeting yourself for the first time, what kind of first impression does your profile give you?

_____

_____

What, if anything, would you add or take out of your profile to improve your first impression?

_____

_____

Facebook Pages You Should Follow

The best Facebook pages to follow are the ones you find yourself: those that cater to your interests and allow you to network with people relevant to the career you want. But there are a handful of pages and groups that every job seeker should take a look at.

Your alumni association

Get connected with your college alumni association. This page can help keep you up to date on news, jobs, networking opportunities, and more.

Professional groups

Search for and identify groups that may be helpful to you professionally, including industry groups, job search communities, and special interests of yours.

Monster.com

Find motivation, tips, and resources for jobs on the Monster.com page: *http://facebook.com/monsterww*

CareerBuilder

CareerBuilder's page offers tips for job seekers, resources for networking, and more.

http://facebook.com/careerbuilder

Social Jobs Partnership

What happens when you combine Facebook, the U.S. Department of Labor, and the National Association of Colleges and Employers? One of the coolest partnerships ever formed: The Social Jobs Partnership. They sponsor live webinars from industry leaders right on their page, as well as up-to-the-minute job search advice. They are also working with Facebook to develop a robust job board, which now boasts over three million jobs

http://facebook.com/socialjobs

Optimizing Twitter for Job Search

Many companies monitor their brand using Twitter. They want to know what people are saying about their products or services. Often times, when you mention a company by name, you'll get a response.

I recently purchased a multi-vitamin from an online herb store. I tweeted about my shopping experience and what a great price I got. That store wrote me back personally to thank me for my business.

Job seekers can take advantage of this "back-door" approach by using Twitter thoughtfully. After all, what other platform lets you communicate directly with hundreds of CEOs, brands, celebrities, recruiters, and reporters in real time?

This workbook isn't the place to convince why you should use Twitter, or the basics of setting up a profile. For this information, turn to my book Job Searching with Social Media For Dummies. Here, you will learn how to use Twitter to network and find a job.

Twitter Is Simple

Twitter doesn't have a whole lot of settings to worry about. The platform was built for simplicity. So here are a handful of simple yet powerful tips for using Twitter to advance your job search.

- Don't protect your tweets. (Check your preferences and make sure this setting is off!)

- Use your LinkedIn picture for consistency.

- Have a customized background and banner for your profile since this is a visual platform.

- Have at least 20 tweets under your belt before you try reaching out.

- Tweet daily. People look at the frequency of your posts to determine how genuine or real you are.

- Follow your target companies; then retweet their posts.

- Follow recruiters, as many as you can; they post jobs often before job boards do.

- Use Twellow.com to find people you want to network with.

I'm Too Old to Tweet

I received a letter from a blog reader who wanted to know if social media really was the way for her to find her next job, because she is of an "older" generation.

> *What are your thoughts regarding Twitter as a tool to finding the next job? I've been hesitant to join and start tweeting (as I'm of an older generation and usually keep my private thoughts/feelings/opinions to myself) but I might just be limiting myself..? What do you think? Any and all suggestions, comments, best practices & critiques are welcome.*

Considering that this whole "generational excuse for not using social media" comes up frequently, I thought I would address her question and help people new to Twitter overcome the resistance they might feel.

Job seekers are turning to social media during the job search.

First of all, let's put the whole age thing aside. I have Boomer clients who don't tweet, and I have Millennial clients who tell me that Twitter is for old people. And between the two of those groups, over 100 million people actively use Twitter. The problem is that Twitter is a platform, and new users expect a solution. Using Twitter without a purpose is much like walking into a bookstore, grabbing a book at random, and then complaining that it didn't help you learn how to change a tire. This can get very frustrating very fast.

Having a purpose when using Twitter will help you avoid all of those people talking about what they had for breakfast or what song they are listening to right now. After all, you control who you follow. And if you are choosing to use Twitter to find a job, then the people you choose to follow will most likely be relevant to your industry and your target organizations.

What you see in your Twitter timeline is 100% correlated with who you follow. If you think the tweets you are seeing are useless, it's because you've followed people posting useless things. This is NOT a reflection of Twitter itself.

According to a recent survey from Jobvite, over 8 million Americans found a job through a connection made via Twitter.

So to answer my reader's question, yes, Twitter is a fundamental tool for the modern job seeker. Avoiding it for whatever reason (pick an excuse) puts you at a significant disadvantage in the marketplace.

Exercise 36: Create Your Real-Time Job Board

Twitter is considered the most popular real-time open network. This means that as items are published, they are immediately available for viewing. And you don't need to follow, connect, or request to see them, making everything posted on Twitter open for you to read.

For job seekers, this is great news because it allows you non-hierarchical access to huge amounts of job information, including postings directly from employers and recruiters.

In order to cut through the fire hose deluge of information and find relevant jobs in your area, create your own customized, real-time job board by following these steps.

1. Log in to Twitter then navigate to http://search.twitter.com

2. Click on Advanced Search to access the hidden search parameters

3. Use one of these words in the field All of these words:

   o   Hiring

   o   Jobs

   o   Jobsearch

4. Enter your city and state abbreviation in the field Near this place

5. Save your search

 To see these steps on a live Twitter account, watch:

http://careerenlightenment.com/wb-twitter-job-board

Discussion

List any exciting job opportunities you found in your area:

_____

_____

Which search terms were more useful than others? Which ones worked best for you?

_____

_____

How did these search results change your willingness to use Twitter?

_____

_____

Exercise 37: Find Five Local Recruiters

On Twitter, you'll find many recruiters and hiring managers tweeting about jobs they're trying to fill. Find five in your area to start following and interacting with.

Here's how you can find them.

Run a simple Google search for Recruiters, Recruiting, Talent Acquisition Firms or Employment Companies in your location.

1. Write down the names of 10.

_____

_____

Log in to Twitter and in the search box on the top of the page, enter the name of one of the recruiters on your list.

2. If his or her Twitter name shows up on Twitter's search results, follow them and say HI!

List five local recruiters that you discovered on Twitter:

Ex. @Bolywelch

@ _____

@ _____

@ _____

@ _____

@ _____

Discussion

What patterns did you notice with the tweets these recruiters post?

_____

_____

What response did you get when you said, "Hi" to the recruiters on your list?

_____

_____

What will you do next to further engage with the top recruiter you found on Twitter?

_____

_____

Exercise 38: Join a Tweetchat

A Twitter Chat, or Tweetchat, is a real-time event that happens over Twitter. It uses a common # (hashtag) in order to tie the conversations together. Typically, the host invites a guest to respond to questions and comments lasting about an hour.

These are opportunities to engage with recruiters and career professionals for advice and networking. They pay more attention to participants who comment and ask questions throughout the full hour.

Find one Tweetchat from the list below to participate in this month and put it on your calendar this week.

To join a Tweetchat, just enter a # (hashtag) into tweetchat.com at the scheduled time.

#JOBHUNTCHAT
Every Monday at 10 p.m. EST

#HFCHAT
Every Friday at noon EST

#CAREERCHAT
Every Tuesday at 1 p.m. EST

#CAREERSAVVY
Tuesdays at 12:30 p.m. EST

#CAREERSUCCESS
Mondays at 8 p.m. EST

#HIREFRIDAY
All day every Friday

#LINKEDINCHAT
Tuesdays at 8 p.m. EST

Discussion

Do a search on Twitter for each of these hashtags. Which stream of tweets interests you the most? Why?

_____

_____

Read through one of these chat streams. What questions would you have asked if you were there live?

Before you go any further, upload your new profile information to your profiles and finish your profile enhancement checklists. Make sure you've got some good-looking profiles before moving forward!

Part 3:
Publish Yourself

Welcome to the World of Publishing

If you're using social media, you are a publisher. Sure, you may not publish scholarly articles on your Facebook page, but you are publishing your own message, your own brand and in your own voice.

By now, you have a firm understanding of your brand message, and you've already transferred that message to your online profiles in a consistent and relevant way. In publishing, this is called a platform. The question is this: Now that you have a platform, what are you going to do with it? Will you let it sit there while you wait for something to happen all the while saying, "social media doesn't work!"? I hope not!

The correct answer: Publish.

Publish your message, communicate with others online so you can talk to them offline, network, and use the voice you've already spent so many hours finding.

> ❝Until he's able to articulate what makes him unique, he'll be right. He won't be different.❞

Roger, a LinkedIn profile writing client, told me that he "wasn't any different than any other accounts payable person out there." And I knew this wasn't true. You see, for someone like Roger, veteran of a single company for 31 years, it might feel like he's not unique. But the truth is that someone sought to keep him around for quite a while. Why? His job search journey will start with him figuring out what makes him unique. Now that he's unemployed, no one else will vouch for him. **Until he's able to articulate what makes him unique, he'd be right. He won't be different.**

Examine the essence of what a hiring manager is looking for and it will come to these three questions:

- Can you do the job?

- Do I like you?

- Are you motivated?

- Although your resume will do a great job answering the first question, it fails to illustrate the last two. Those questions are about your personality. And the great thing is, there can only be one you. Your voice, your opinions, your likes and dislikes, your successes, your experiences, your innate abilities all contribute to who you are as a worker. The faster and more effectively you can communicate answers to all three questions, the faster you will get hired.

Social media offers you a free and easy way to share your voice. Many people feel uncomfortable sharing publicly at first. However with practice, you may find that the more you share who you are with the world, the more confident you will feel about yourself. You do have valuable things to say. And you will find, over time, that other people value what you have to say.

This next section will guide you through your first posts online and give you the frameworks you need to stay engaged and begin conversations with influential people in your target organizations.

What Do You Say?

A common fear when people begin to consider publishing through social media is "I just don't have anything to say." So does that mean that when you are hanging out with your friends, you just sit there, mute? Probably not. Everyone has a voice. Some people's digital voices are simply not well practiced. To get you started with figuring out what to say, here is a short list of possible topics.

- An industry related article

- A quote you found relevant or inspiring

- A question you have for your audience

- An opinion you'd like to ask about something

- A picture of yourself at a hobby or professional event

- Advice you have for someone else

- An insight

- An opinion

- A frustration

- A link to a company

- A re-shareing of someone else's post

- Sharing your job search progress

- Telling people what you are looking for

In the screenshot below, Orietta does a nice job pulling a powerful quote from an article she read. She's able to solicit comments from her network and start a conversation.

Orietta E. Ramirez commented on a discussion in Career Attraction - www.careerattraction.com.

"You manage tasks, but you lead people"

Management Is (Still) Not Leadership - Harvard Business Review

A few weeks ago, the BBC asked me to come in for a radio interview.

Like (1) · Comment (4) · 1 hour ago

Douglas McMurray

Show previous comments

Douglas McMurray Very insightful, the author clarifies something I think a lot of us "leaders" are guilty of misconstruing. Thank you for starting this thread.
3 hours ago

Orietta E. Ramirez Barbara - I would be curious to know what you found you needed to improve upon with respect to your management skills, and how your leadership qualities could enhance the process. Douglas, very true, there is a gray area when defining what leaders do... more
1 hour ago

Levels of Language

While most people imagine a very formal job search language for resumes and cover letters, writing on social media can be much more casual, more authentic, and more narrative in style.

Consider this major shift in language when using social media: that the very best LinkedIn profiles are written in the first person. I've heard many stories of people shifting this one element and getting fabulous results online.

As a terrible speller myself, it always irks me to hear how picky many employers are with typos and spelling errors. What a shallow judge of character! But the reality is that on your more formal job search documents, resume, email inquiry (cover letter), or job application, spelling and grammatical mistakes can ruin your chances. Luckily, you don't have to be so uptight when writing for social media. Especially when you are sending out posts.

Most people understand that there is a fine balance between the timeliness of the post (getting it out fast) and the quality of the post (how it is written). The more you post, the better your digital literacy; you will be able to post faster with more quality posts but only with practice. At first, however, you may feel the urge to hold onto your words like a mother reluctant to let her first-born drive off to college for the first time. It's natural.

Here are some tips to help you with your first posts:

- Always write in the first person, using I or me, rather that he or she.

- The shorter the lifespan of your post, the less you have to worry about proper writing. For example, Tweets, Timeline Posts, and LinkedIn Updates don't even need to be in complete sentences. If a typo happens, it's okay.

- Longer lifespan content should be more polished. For example, your Facebook About You section, Twitter Bio, or LinkedIn Profile should be free of typos and spelling. Grammar can be of the truncated sort.

- If you can say it in fewer words, do so. Brevity is the key when communicating online.

- If you can say it with a picture, do so. Remember the old proverb: "A picture is worth 1,000 words."

- Don't $ell, YELL, or be a troll. Imagine one person in front of you, and you are simply starting a conversation with them. Write down what you might say to that one person.

Exercise 39: Try Your First Posts

Try writing down your first posts in this workbook, so only you can see them. Then venture out into the wild-wild-west (WWW) and see what the cowboys say. Don't be shy here. Imagine you are reading your LinkedIn home page looking for interesting comments from other people in your network. What might you say? Is there an article you might link to and then comment on?

To help you think of something to say, imagine you are at a party and you've bumped into someone you know. What might you say to him or her?

1. Does it show your voice or are you just passing along information?

2. Is it interesting to your target audience?

3. Is your personal brand clear?

4. Does it show your motivation and personality?

Now you try. Write down your first posts on all three platforms here.

1. LinkedIn Status Update (700 Character Limit)—The Cocktail Party

Quote of the day: "I found one!" SASHA ZAREZINA, 8, searching a snow bank in Deputatskoye, Russia, for fragments of a meteor.

Now you try…

_____

_____

2. Facebook Timeline Post (146-420 Character Limit)—The After Party

When I was having my Starbucks the other day, I overheard some project managers talking about a late project and poor team dynamics. It always makes me sad to hear that. I remember when I had to turn around a team that didn't gel. Was one of the most rewarding work experiences of my life!

Now you try…

_____

_____

3. Twitter Tweet (140 Character Limit)—The Holiday Party

Just noticed the days are getting longer. February, you may be cold, but you can't stop my optimism!

Now you try…

Discussion

How is posting online different than an in-person conversations?

_____

_____

After you finished your first post, did it seem to go easier?

_____

_____

What changed knowing you were on LinkedIn versus Facebook or Twitter?

_____

_____

Now go forth and post! (or mingle, take your pick)

Exercise 40: Your Daily Social Media 20-Minute Ritual

If you're concerned about getting sucked into social media and spending too much time here, use these daily rituals to limit yourself. Simply run down this checklist each day to be sure you've covered all of your bases. Then you can decide to play around in each network—or grab a latté.

You can print a copy of this ritual and stick it next to your desk to help you manage your time. Here's a nice looking version for you: *http://careerenlighten-ment.com/20-minute-ritual-pinup*

Right now, do a practice run of your ritual. Go through each network, follow the steps listed. Do this today, and tomorrow and every day this week until you don't have to look at this list anymore.

Run through the following steps now.

Download Your Ritual

Remember to download a nice looking version of the social media ritual here:

http://careerenlightenment.com/20-minute-ritual-pinup

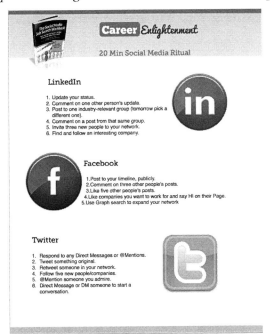

Login to LinkedIn

- Update your status, say something to your network.

- Comment on one other person's update.

- Post to one industry-relevant group (tomorrow pick a different one).

- Comment on a post from that same group.

- Invite at least three new people to your network.

- Find and follow an interesting company or thought leader.

Login to Facebook

- Post to your public timeline, setting the audience to Public.

- Comment on three other people's posts.

- Like five other people's posts.

- Like companies you want to work for and say HI on their Page.

Login to Twitter

- Respond to any Direct Messages or @Mentions.

- Tweet something original.

- Retweet someone in your network.

- Follow five new people/companies.

- @Mention someone you admire.

- Direct Message or DM someone to start a conversation.

The FIRE Method Overview

Ever heard of the "hidden job market"? It's a term thrown around but is actually very misleading. There is no stone you can lift up to reveal this "hidden" depository of jobs. There are, however, techniques you can use to gain access to the 80% of jobs that are never posted on public job boards. The FIRE method is one such technique, and one that my clients have used successfully since 2010.

The **FIRE** method, which you're about to learn, is designed to give you the maximum exposure to key contacts within an organization while arming you with the information you need to make a great first impression with decision makers who are looking for someone just like you.

FIRE stands for:

- Find

- Identify

- Reach out

- Engage

This method is technology agnostic. Use what ever social media tools that work to achieve each step. Sure, LinkedIn will play a large role. But so will Facebook, Twitter, and what ever other tool you deem relevant to your industry or in your location.

It's a great feeling when you can find jobs you are interested in on job boards. It feels even better when you click *Apply*. You did something tangible towards getting a job! But it doesn't feel good when you don't hear anything back, or when, after a few weeks, you get a form rejection letter.

As Peter Drucker famously said, "Efficiency is doing things right; effectiveness is doing the right things."

Trolling job boards is NOT doing the right thing, i.e. job board applications are not the most effective use of your time.

When career advisers tell you to get informational interviews, it's not just about the information; it's about the relationships you are building. And with social media, it's also about those second- and third-degree connections into a target organization that you gain access to.

Kathy, a Career Enlightenment blog reader, was unemployed and really wanted to work as a project manager at Symantec, the big software company. Of course she looked at job board listings, but mainly she used LinkedIn and Twitter to build connections with people there.

> **❝Most job seekers are opportunistic. They wait for job openings and then apply— along with the 118 others. By using the FIRE method, you're doing more than your competition is likely to do.❞**

After several months of informational interviews, coffee meetings, follow-up calls, and emails, her networking finally paid off. One of her job boards sent her an alert about Symantec's open project manager role in her city. Excited, she contacted one of her closest new friends from LinkedIn, informed her that she just applied, and she'd appreciate it if she would let HR know.

Her contact called HR to make an internal referral, and in a matter of days, she got a call. Six weeks later, she started her dream job.

Did she use a job board? Sure! But she relied on the networking technique I'm about to share with you: the FIRE method.

(F) Find companies and people you wish to target

In this step of the **FIRE** method—**Find**—you will look for companies you want to work for, regardless of their job openings. After all, most jobs never get listed on job boards!

What you are **Finding** is a specific list of not just companies but also people of interest, or POI at those companies. Job seekers often forget that human beings make hiring decisions, not machines.

The types of POI you should look for are:

- Possible decision makers, like managers, directors, VPs

- Possible informational interview sources, people with the same titles you have, or who work along side that title

- Alumni or other connections in your target industry or company with a commonality (school, hometown, causes, hobbies etc.)

The better you understand who the key players are, the better you can tailor your message to their needs. Furthermore, if you wait for the job to get posted, you're already too late. That's why I suggest you build a list of companies that interest you, regardless of their published opportunities.

> ❝Efficiency is doing things right; effectiveness is doing the right things.❞
>
> — Peter Drucker

You'll do this by triangulating, from the highest level, the industry you want to work for, down to the smallest level, the POI at each company.

The Find step is accomplished by:

1. Looking at your industry of interest and location of interest

2. Building a list of 10 companies to target at a time

3. Recording POIs for each company

Now it's time for you to build your Hit List. The more specific you get now, the easier things will be for you later.

Exercise 41: Fill in Your Hit List

In order for you to complete your hit list, you'll need to use social media tools. Reach the instructions for each of the three major networks to learn how to do this.

Using LinkedIn's Company Search

For video instruction, watch:
http://careerenlightenment.com/wb-top-10-companies

1. Visit LinkedIn's list of industries and find the one that best matches you: *http://careerenlightenment.com/industry-list*

2. Set the filters to the location where you want to find a job, to more details about the industry, and to the size of the ideal company. Your goal is a list of ten companies you're interested in.

3. Clicking on one of your target companies, find POIs, that might be a potential hiring manager or information source. Enter those into the table below.

Using Zoominfo

For video instruction, watch:
http://careerenlightenment.com/wb-zoominfo

1.   Create a free *Zoominfo.com* account.

2.   Start a new search, choosing the Companies tab.

3.   Enter the industry and location you are interested in pursuing

4.   Click on the People link to see who works there and record your results below.

Using LinkedIn's Alumni Tool

For video instruction, watch:
http://careerenlightenment.com/wb-linkedin-alumni

1. Visit *linkedin.com/alumni*

2. Choose your school and begin using the filters.

3. Find alumni working in the field or city you're interested in pursuing and record them below.

Using Facebook Graph Search

For video instruction, watch:
http://careerenlightenment.com/wb-facebook-graph-search

Using the search bar at the top of your Facebook page, called Graph Search, use the following search strings.

1. People who work at (company) who live in (location)

2. People who work at (company) who went to (school)

3. Friends of my friends who work at (company)

4. Companies my friends like who live in (location)

Using the tools outlined above to complete this table.

Industry	Company	Person of Interest

(I) Identify the company's needs and the person's needs

In this step of the FIRE method—Identify—you will research each industry, company, and contact from your Hit List in order to understand their needs, goals, and challenges.

Corporations are not people (no jokes about Mit, please!). Point is, people hire you, actual living breathing (suffering, emotional, goal oriented people) not emotionless, brainless corporations. People make hiring decisions in a very human way, that is, based on split-second impressions. That's why when you are making those first impressions online, it's important that your message hit home right away.

Your goal in this step is to identify what these target people are thinking about, worried about, or aspiring to, so that when you reach out to them, your message shines out through all the rest of the clutter they're probably filtering in their head.

Identify the needs, goals, or challenges of your target organization and the people on your Hit List.

Exercise 42: Message Targeting Analysis

Use the following resources to gather information about your target companies and POIs; then record it in the table below.

 For video instruction on how to conduct this research, watch: *http:// careerenlightenment.com/wb-company-needs*

Industry Information Sources

alltop.com: This is a great site for getting industry-specific news and information.

News.google.com: Look for news about the industry, company, or person to see what issues could be pressing on them right now.

LinkedIn Groups: By joining and following active LinkedIn groups for your industry, you can see quickly what people are talking about the most. Try filtering the discussions by Most Popular.

Company Information Sources

LinkedIn Company Page: Look at the company's most recent updates on their company page, look at who their competition is, look at their style of posting, etc.

Facebook Pages: Get a sense of the company culture and style by looking at their Facebook page, even better, if they have a page just for recruiting. If you can find the personal Facebook profile of the people on your hit list, see how much information they've made public. There might be some thing you have in common.

Official Tweets: Look at the company's last 20 tweets and see what the tone is and what topics are discussed. Can you find the tweets of the people on your hit list? These are gold!

POI Information Sources

Imagine: Refer to your personal branding profile from Part 1. If you were in their shoes, what goals would you have, what challenges would you be facing?

Personal Tweets: Try to find your POI on Twitter. Are they active? If so, pay attention to what they are talking about. Record any insights.

LinkedIn Status Updates or Articles: Does your POI post status updates or write articles published on LinkedIn? If so, record their topics, goals, pains and interests.

Google Search: Search for their name with quotes around it in a Google search. Find anything interesting?

Using the tools above, record your research in this table.

Industry/Company/POI	Interests	Goals or Pain

(R) Reach for Informational Interviews

In this step of the **FIRE** method—**Reach out**—you will interview information sources to network, to validate your research and to test your assumptions.

No matter how much research you do on your own, nothing will serve you more than having live conversations with a POI in your target industry or in your target company. These days, networks are large enough that it's not uncommon to have several second-degree connections in your target organization. Leverage your network to set up low-pressure informational interviews to validate your understanding of the industry and company.

Kathy, remember her from last section, info-interviewed for her role at Symantec for over two months. She learned about the company's culture, their direction, and possible areas of growth. Then when her dream job opened up, she was able to call on her info-interview relationships to flag her application. She made it to first-round interviews because she asked questions and connected with people in the company. She got hired because she was a great fit for the job.

First, you need to find possible informational interview sources, or someone of a parallel position willing to talk to you.

A Case Study For Getting Info Interviews on LinkedIn

Here's a sample info interview request inMail and my analysis of what makes it so good:

Hi Joshua,

I noticed that we are both connected to M. F. – how do you know M.? I first met her at Jacob's Pillow, and she actually photographed my wedding. Small world!

I wanted to touch base with you because I saw an open position at J.R. that I thought would be a great fit for me. I'm located in Portland now (after being in Massachusetts and DC for many years), and do social media strategy for a digital marketing agency here in town.

It's a fun role, but you know how agencies are – fingers in a lot of different businesses, but no ability to truly own a marketing program. It looks like I would be able to do that with the Marketing Communications Manager role that is posted.

Would you mind if I called you sometime this week to hear about your experience at J.R. and your perspective on the marketing organization there? I'd really appreciate it.

Regards,

Lead with something in common

J began his email by pointing out our mutual friend M. F. And although I know M. F. from my sister's college days, what really got my attention was that M. F. was the photographer on her wedding too.

Now, with LinkedIn, there is a danger that the first-degree connection isn't really a close friend. I went through an Open Networking phase, and about 100 people in my LinkedIn network are complete strangers to me.

So don't assume that just because they're connected, they know each other.

J. took a calculated risk. However, he mitigates that risk by further sharing a personal tidbit…he's married. And as another recently married guy, I can very much relate to his situation.

The lesson is that leading with a commonality is best. Did you go to the same school, are you from the same hometown, do you share the same hobbies, or maybe it's a connection as loose as simply being part of the same LinkedIn group.

Get to the point, fast

J wastes no time in BS or apologies. He's writing to me because he saw an open position at a company I have a relationship with and thinks he'd be a fit.

Notice he says, "I saw an open position." He doesn't assume I know anything about this position. In fact, it was news to me. And so I can infer that he's not assuming I'm any kind of decision maker. I know this is going to be a purely informational interview.

Furthermore, he concludes the email by re-affirming that he's just looking to hear about my experience with J. R., the company, and my perspective on their marketing organization.

My guard goes down because I know he's not going to put me on the spot or ask me for more than my opinion.

What makes him qualified for the role he's interested in?

Without bragging, J makes it clear that he's a serious candidate for the role he mentions, not a job fisherman.

He tells me he already works at an agency. And even though he enjoys the agency, he's looking for more. He wants to "truly own a marketing program."

It might occur to me, after all, that if he already has a job, why is he looking to make a change? That concern is assuaged.

What do you want from me?

He concludes his email with "Would you mind if I called you sometime this week…" meaning I won't have to do anything except wait for a phone call and talk to him. Sounds easy.

If I had sent the email to a prospective interview, I would have also mentioned the exact amount of time such a conversation would take: "Would you mind if I called you this week for just 10 or 15 minutes?"

Other observations

You may have also noticed that:

- The email was VERY short. It took me less than 30 seconds to read it.

- He named the position he was after by name, he did his research, and I sense he won't waste my time.

- He is sensitive to and grateful for my time: "I would really appreciate it…"

A note on conducting the info interview:

People know right away if you aren't prepared. Be prepared to lead the conversation through questions you've written down and thought about. Specifically, you should ask questions around these three areas:

- What is going well for them at the company?

- What is frustrating or challenging for them right now?

- Who else can you talk to at the company to get the information you need?

How to Get Info Interviews Using Facebook

Facebook provides you with several powerful networking tools. The first is Graph Search, where you can find just about anyone you can imagine. The second is Paid Messages, where you can pay to have your message sent to the person of your choice, regardless of connection.

Here's how to use these tools.

Graph Search

Find the person you want to connect with for information interviews. These could be people working in specific roles within a target company, or an alum working within a target industry.

At the top of your Facebook page in the search bar, try these searches:

1. People who work at (company) who live in (location)

2. People who work at (company) who went to (school)

3. Friends of my friends who work at (company)

 For video instruction, watch:
http://careerenlightenment.com/wb-facebook-graph-search

Paid Messages

After you've found the person you want to talk to for the informational interview, use the Message feature to connect with him or her.

If it's someone you are connected with through a friend, you won't have to pay for a message. If the person is completely unconnected to you, your message will show up in their "Other" folder unless you pay. And since no one checks the "Other" folder, you will want to pay. Chances are you've never even looked in your Other folder!

 For instructions, watch:
http://careerenlightenment.com/wb-facebook-paid-message

Most paid messages cost between $1 and $10 to send (see screenshot previous page).

What to Say

Since you are networking professionally, follow the same principles you would follow when connecting through LinkedIn.

- Lead with something in common.

- Get to the point fast.

- Build credibility.

- Make an easy call to action.

Here's an example:

Hi Sandra,

I found your Facebook profile when looking for other project managers working at Target. Your profile came up in my search. I hope you don't mind that I've reached out.

I'm currently looking for work, but don't worry, this is not a job solicitation. I'm just looking to learn more about what it's like to work at Target to see if I'd be a fit or not. As an experienced project manager, I know fit is extremely important for a successful career. That's why I'd like to connect with you.

Would you be open to chatting with me for about 15 minutes next Thursday? I've prepared some questions and getting your feedback would be extremely helpful for me in deciding whether to apply to Target.

Would you be available at 4pm next Thursday?

Thanks in advance for your time!

Gitta Kwainted

How to Get Info Interviews Using Twitter

Despite Twitter's simplicity, cutting through the clutter and getting someone's attention can be a bit of a journey.

After you've found the person you'd like to have an informational interview with, begin interacting with him or her.

Here is a process I've used to successfully get the attention of busy people via Twitter:

Day 1. Retweet something they said to your own audience and then follow them.

Day 2. Use an @reply to share an interesting article with them.

Day 3. @Reply to them with a simple question or a message that invokes curiosity, for example, "What does Vegetarian Gym Rat mean in your bio?" or "I just read a new book about product marketing that you might like."

Day 4. Continue until they follow you back.

As soon as they follow you back, Direct Message them to try to get a meeting offline. For example, "I'm visiting SF next week and would love to meet up for coffee. Do you have time?"

Exercise 43: Tracking Your Networking Progress

Using the social media tools outlined above for networking, complete the table below.

POI	Channel	Date	Response	Next Step
Ex. John Adams	InMail	12/15	Replied 12/18	Meeting for coffee next week
Sally Gabsalot	Twitter @ reply	12/16	No reply	@reply again next week

(E) Engage with the decision-maker

In this step of the **FIRE** method—**Engage**—you will reach out to the decision maker of your target company to set up a time to meet.

I met Jacob at a Brown University Alumni summer picnic in Oregon. He told me he was moving to San Francisco with the hope of getting a job. I suggested that he change his goal from getting a job to just getting to know people at companies he was interested in. A few months later I bumped into Jacob at a food cart during a conference lunch break. There he was, having lunch with his new boss, whom he met by asking her to lunch just for networking. He told me, "About half-way through our conversation, I felt it shift from casual networking to 'job interview questions.'" You never know when your networking will turn into a job interview.

Remember, this is all about relationships. Approximately 50% to 75% of the time, when you connect with potential hiring managers in a respectful way like this, approaching through common interests and concerns, it will eventually turn into an hour-long interview, and then they recommend you to someone else if the fit is not right. Relationships are built that way.

When you are making your initial contact, don't be afraid to offer help. If it's not something you can help him or her with, you can always say, "You know, I don't think that is something that I can help you with, but I do know someone who would be a perfect fit for that problem or that opportunity for you. Would you like me to connect the two of you?" There's nothing wrong with offering help and providing value to someone in your network.

Exercise 44: Decision-Maker Topic Index

In the table below, fill in the company you are targeting, the name of the decision-maker, what you think his or her needs are, and how you can help him or her. This cheat sheet will help you when you write your first email to them a bit later on. Remember to use your newfound social media research chops to answer these questions.

Company	POI	Their Need	How You Can Help

Exercise 45: Craft Your Message to Hiring Managers

Now craft your first message to the decision maker. Remember that you are not asking for a job; rather, you are wanting to see if there could be a fit. Keep your request for time short and specific. Refer back to the lessons in the **Reach Out** section on how to write a communication that gets replies.

Typically, you'll want to use LinkedIn to make this first approach. But this will depend on your industry. In some cases, as in marketing or PR, Twitter often creates a better first impression. It's important to strategically decide which channel you will use.

Here's a LinkedIn inMail template you can make your own. For more templates, visit: *http://careerenlightenment.com/linkedin-inmail-templates*

Hi Christina,

I ran across your profile on LinkedIn because I'm looking for marketing opportunities at (target company). I've been following the fast growth of the company over the last 3 years and want to see if there may be a place for me to help out.

I know there may not be open opportunities at the moment, just so I'm not wasting your time or mine, I'd love a chance to speak with you about the company and see if I might, one day, be a fit.

II received an (name your degree) from XXX University and have spent the last 3 years working in sales and marketing for (name past company).

I specialized in (your elevator pitch).

I promise not to take any more than 15-20 minutes of your time. Will you have some time this week for a chat? I have Thursday at 9am and Friday at 2pm available.

Looking forward to your reply,

Gitta Kwainted

Exercise 46: Decision-Maker Networking Tracking

Keep track of your communications with hiring managers here.

Company	POI Name	Needs/ problems/ goals/interests	Commonalities	Channel Used	Date of Contact	Response	Next step

Managing Your Online Reputation

If the statistics are true, 80% of employers will Google you. So run your job search under the assumption that you will get googled. The question is this: How do you maximize that online image of yourself so that you are seen in the best possible light? While, in the past, gaps in your work history were a big deal, today questionable online content is a bigger deal. This section will show you not just how to get rid of unwanted content about you online but also how to build an online reputation that sells you to employers.

To manage your online reputation, follow these ABCs:

1. Assess it

How good or how bad is it? What's your diagnosis? Based on this information, you'll be able to better determine your course of action. Unfortunately, repairing or even building an online reputation does take time.

2. Build or repair it

The best way to get rid of the stuff that you don't want out there is to create new stuff to bury the old stuff. (Yes, stuff is a technical term!)

3. Care for it

Remember that managing your career doesn't just happen every three to four years when you change jobs. Managing your career should be a consistent part of your professional life until you retire. This is your brand. It will carry you into the next position. It will pick you up from unemployment. Your brand is going to communicate and grow throughout your career.

Exercise 47: Assessing Your Online Reputation

To know how hard to work on building your Google resume, you first have to know where you currently stand. Follow the next activities to get a better sense.

1. Get Your Google grade

 To see this process in action, watch: *http://careerenlightenment.com/wb-google-grade*

Google your "name in quotation marks"; then answer the following questions:

On the three pages of results, how many times does an accurate reference to you show up? Record your answers here:

_____**out of**_____ total results on 3 pages (example: 20 references to me out of 30 total results)

On the three pages of results, how many times does a negative reference to you show up?

_____ (example: there were 2 negative references)

Sum the above for Your Grade_____ (example: 20-2=18 good results. 18/30=60% or a D)

2. Perform a Manual Self-screening

Public records often reveal more about you than you ever intended. Use the following sites to search your name and see if there is information about you. Record whether that information is accurate here.

Search Engine	Results
Pipl.com	
Zoominfo.com	
Spokeo.com	

If any of the information is inaccurate, you have a right to email the site's customer service and have it either removed or corrected.

Exercise 48: Building Your Online Reputation

Customize Domains with Your Name

Google determines what search results rise to the top based on something that they call Authority. Other search engines use different criteria, but that's not important right now. That's because Google has 80% market share and typically what comes up on Google comes up on the other search engines.

Some sites have more authority than others. For example, LinkedIn has more authority than many other sites. That's why changing your LinkedIn profile URL to your own name results in an almost instant ranking for your profile.

Websites with your name in the URL or domain name are also considered higher authority. This is why when you purchase your domain name as your name, like joshuawaldman.net, that page tends to rank. Anyone looking to control his or her Google resume should own his or her own domain name! Let's do that now.

 Learn how to buy your domain name and set up a website here: *http://careerenlightenment.com/jobseekers-website-setup*

What is your custom LinkedIn domain name? (Does it include your name?)

What is your personal domain name? Do you have a website installed yet?

Exercise 49: Repurpose your body of work

Creating new content solely for the sake of ranking in Google can be quite frustrating. If you have a blog, this is easy. However, most people don't have a blog (nor do they want one). So the next best option is to publish content you've already developed on Google-indexed sharing sites.

- Articles, essays, papers, reports go on Scribd or docstoc

- Videos go on Youtube or Vimeo

- Presentations go on Slideshare

- Photos go on Flickr or Picassaweb

- Portfolios of creative work go on Behance or Carbonmade

Fill in the following worksheet to see if this strategy will work for you. First, write down descriptions or titles of any written works you have authored. These could be articles, papers, or reports. Do the same for any presentation slides you've built, any videos you've either been in or filmed, and any pictures of you.

Write down as many of these as you have for each category.

Writings	Slides	Videos	Pictures	Portfolio

Exercise 50: Your Content Calendar

It's not a good idea to publish everything all at one time. A better strategy is to release your content slowly over the course of one or two months.

So, use the table below to decide when you will post your content on the appropriate sharing sites.

Week	Writings	Slides	Videos	Pictures	Portfolio
Week 1					
Week 2					
Week 3					
Week 4					

Exercise 51: Care for Your Online Reputation

Online reputation management isn't a one-time project. As long as the Internet is around, you will need to care for and maintain your reputation. Luckily, this isn't difficult.

The easiest way to keep up your online reputation is with a free tool from Google called Google Alerts. Every time Google indexes something with your name, or with whatever keyword you use, it sends you an alert either via email or RSS.

 For detailed video instruction, watch: *http://careerenlightenment.com/wb-google-alerts*

1. Visit: *http://alerts.google.com*

2. Enter your name as the search term in quotation marks.

3. Decide how often you want to get alerts.

You can also set up similar alerts with *http://www.socialmention.com*

Theoretically, when you publish new content online, either a blog post, an article, video, or whatever, within a day or so, you should get an alert from Google telling you that it was indexed. It's a simple tool.

I also suggest you create a schedule for yourself and Google yourself monthly or quarterly. Note the progress you're making with your publishing campaign, and see who's talking about you out there. If something isn't right, you'll know right away and be able to respond.

What Google Alerts have you set up?

_____

_____

Commit to Your Google Schedule:

I will Google myself every (an interval that works for you) _____.

I will help myself remember to do these searches by (list your favorite method of creating automated reminders) _____ .

I will search on the following variations on my name (list various ways people might refer to you): _____

You Made It...

66 ...here are some parting thoughts **99**

If this work were easy, everyone would do it and there would be no unemployment! So take a breath and acknowledge your huge accomplishment of getting through this workbook. In these pages, you have uncovered your deepest personal brand and found strong and compelling ways to communicate it online so that employers will be magnetized to you.

The average job seeker will skip to the fun stuff (like the LinkedIn profile tweaks) without recognizing that Facebook offers a higher probability of getting hired or that their cross-platform messaging will be inconsistent without planning. Your hard work will pay off.

As you've probably already discovered, the biggest hurdle to running a successful social media job search is your own willingness to do the work. And for most people, resistance comes from not having clear next steps or a clear vision of what the end will look like. It is my intention that the course and this workbook will have dissolved those hurdles giving you a clear goal and easy steps to get there.

In your career, these three P's—Positioning|Polishing|Publishing—will manifest themselves in many ways. They certainly apply to your job search. You might also find that they work with creating and marketing a new product, getting out of a PR emergency, or saving an account from turning upside down.

I don't know how fast you will get your next job. And I don't know how soon you will see results from following these three P's. I can promise you that they work. Following them, your job search will feel easier, more fluid. You don't need to spend hours scouring job boards or stressing out about your resume. You just need to position, polish, and publish who you are.

Good Luck On Your Job Search!

Additional Resources

For those of you interested in staying up to date on social media, job search, or both, here are some resources worth looking into.

Mashable.com offers intelligent and up-to-date news and opinion on social media topics, including frequent pieces on modern job seeking and recruiting.

Smartbrief.com/socialmedia is an email service where the most important social media news gets emailed directly to you so you don't have to go out and find it.

Careerenlightenment.com is a website dedicated to synthesizing social media and technology in a way that makes sense to job seekers. Sign up to get access to a weekly newsletter and video training.

Liprofile.com is a premier LinkedIn profile writing service I run with ten of the country's top profile writers whom I've trained to provide you with a job-attracting online profile within a week. We offer basic profile services plus Spanish language profiles as well as services for re-entering veterans and government jobs.

Careerrocketeer.com publishes articles from the country's top career experts. They strive to bring you new ways to think about your job search and career.

Job-hunt.org spends a lot of time finding the best writers and thinkers to give you an authoritative resource for your career. The site also has job club directories and many free e-books for download.

CareerAttraction.com Career Attraction provides actionable advice, tips, and hacks from leading job search and career experts.

About the Author

PHOTO BY AJ COOTS

Joshua Waldman is an author, speaker, and trainer specializing in helping people regain control of their careers in today's tough economic and technology climate. As the author of the best-selling **Job Searching with Social Media For Dummies**, he enjoys presenting keynotes and workshops on personal branding, online reputation, and advanced LinkedIn strategy. He also runs CareerEnlightenment.com, a successful career blog.

Joshua's interest in social media career advancement combines his lifelong passion for technology and his extensive training in job search strategy as an MBA. When he got laid off twice in six months and bounced right back into good jobs, he realized that his philosophy and strategies were powerful enough to help the careers of others. This experience, combined with 5 years as a social media strategist, career consultant, and blogger, gives him a unique perspective on these online job search techniques. It is Joshua's hope that by sharing his knowledge, others will regain a sense of control over their careers, find clarity on how to use social media more effectively in the long term, and rekindle their passion for why they got into their industry in the first place.

Joshua earned a BA at Brown University in 2000. Since then, he has earned an MBA from Boston University's International Management Program. He sits on the board of the National Speakers Association in Oregon.

Joshua lives in Portland, Oregon, with his wife, their teenage daughter, and their Pomeranian, Boy-Boy. When not working, Joshua likes to experiment with vegetarian cooking, losing at the game of Go, working out at CrossFit gyms, and going for walks in the Northwest badlands. He can be reached on Twitter at *@joshuawaldman*, LinkedIn at *http://linkedin.com/in/joshuawaldman*, or via email at *joshua@careerenlightenment.com*.

"Job Searching with Social Media For Dummies" is the Perfect Companion Book!

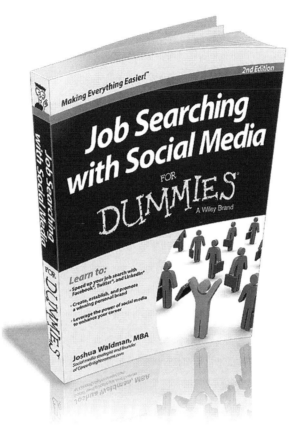

What People Other Than My Mom Are Saying!

"This book lays out how to assemble and execute a social media strategy, clearly and cleanly, so you can be competitive and cut-short your job search. I'm grateful to have it on my desk as a reference/resource for my fellow career coaches and job seekers!"

– Susan Whitcomb, Resume Writer

"Current job seekers need to be aware of these new strategies to find a job."

– Douglas Andrews, Career Coach

"This book will teach you what you need to know ... not just to get by, but to excel."

– Arthur Fewell, Now Gainfully Employed

Read over 100 reviews on Amazon!

Not Happy with Results You're Getting on LinkedIn?

Let a Professional Profile Writer Help Get You Noticed!

You should be getting weekly calls from recruiters.

You're not?

Then you're profile needs some polish!

"Joshua's LinkedIn Profile service was extremely easy to use and very helpful. The process started with a questionnaire and after I uploaded my resume, within 36 hours I received my completed profile"

– Libby Neison

"My LinkedIn profile is by far more professional and polished now more than most others I have seen! The follow-up support and recommended actions alone are worth the fee.

– Katherin Bacon

"It was a pleasure to work with Career Enlightenment while they fine tuned my LinkedIn profile. The order process was easy and the entire profile was done within the promised 48 hours. I highly recommend this excellent resource to help you look your best on LinkedIn."

– Maria Ferre

For an exclusive offer for Workbook readers visit:

http://liprofile.com

This Workbook Comes With An Instructors Manual!

Rather than reinventing the wheel every time you teach a social media jobs skills workshop, why not use a proven program used across the country for thousands of job seekers?

In the Instructors Manual, you'll get access to:

• A done-for-you syllabus for two, two hour sessions using this very workbook

• Detailed lecture notes, slides and in-classroom activities

• Access to online supplemental technical lessons, so you don't have to teach technology

To learn about purchase options, visit:

http://careerenlightenment.com/facilitators

Professional social media training, so you don't have to!

Joshua Waldman's programs would make an excellent companion to your current career skills curriculum.

Joshua teaches around the country and would be glad to speak with you about how you can use him to augment your professional development programing.

Typical programs include:

- Keynotes for job seekers and professionals

- Train-the-trainer workshops for career coaches and advisors

"My team said you were the most valuable speaker we ever had. My goal was to raise their awareness and their job search techniques vocabulary. You did that and more!"

Madeleine Slutsky, Vice President Student & Career Services, *DeVry University*

To download Joshua's brochure visit careerenlightenment.com/speaking, or contact him at 503-985-6741 or bookings@careerenlightenment.com

Made in the USA
Columbia, SC
26 November 2017